Transitions 2

*Kelly —
Thank you for the great job on my back cover!
Jean Long Manteufel*

What people are saying:

"Jean captures the wisdom and experiences of people through their stories. She is able to express what really matters most to our loved ones and puts into words what is on the person's heart."

- Chris J. Mares, Estate Planning Attorney

"I am a BIG fan of Jean's work – the messages are incredibly helpful and make a significant difference."

**- Cathie Tierney, President, CEO
Community First Credit Union**

"Jean's columns provide real life situations, thought provoking questions and helpful tips to guide families through transitions during these seasons of life. Her book, <u>Transitions</u>, is a guiding light to help loved ones work through it together."

**- Lori M. Coonen, HDP, Family Legacy Coach
Living My Legacy**

"Our world has become more complex and filled with information. Jean has a unique talent for creating poignant, relevant thoughts on older adult topics, with brevity. I have learned from Jean's expertise and guidance both personally and professionally. Her words ring true. A must read!"

- Bobbie Thompson, Brookdale Appleton

"As a lifelong antique dealer, I deal with the issues Jean addresses on a daily basis, which is why I am buying 4 copies of this book, one for each of my children. This whole aging thing is going to be a breeze, thanks to Jean."

-Greg Willett, Owner
Greg Willett Antiques and Estate Sales Services

"They say 'tug at the heart to open the mind'. I've long enjoyed reading Jean's columns for her heartfelt messages that inspire me to do more. Jean shares her personal experience in a way that recalls our own fond memories of family and friends. Her advice is simple and easy to act on, but most importantly, meaningful to the loved ones around us. Whether you've shared similar experiences or are about to, you'll find Jean's columns touch your heart."

– Joel Hopper, Vice President, Hands of Time

"Jean's book has been a valuable resource manual for the elderly people in our lives. My husband and I also use the book to help us prepare as we are thinking about retiring. We don't want to leave all that cleaning out of our junk just because we think there is some attachment to our belongings. Our kids have said, "No thanks!" There is some very sound advice in the book; you just have to follow it."

- Beth Davis, Ambassador
Fox Cities Chamber of Commerce

Transitions 2

Stories of how to get help when you are overwhelmed

Jean Long Manteufel

Illustrations by Gladie Long and Laura Long Muinde

Cover design by Sam Needham

Copyright © 2019   Jean Long Manteufel

First edition, first printing

All rights reserved

ISBN: 9781079134292
Independently published

No part of this book may be used or reproduced in any manner without written permission except in the case of brief excerpts used in reviews.

Library of Congress Control Number: 2019910054
Grandma Fav Publishing, Appleton WI

(920)734-3260
TransitionsWithJean.com

DEDICATION

To my hubby, Randy
– You give me wings to fly. Yeah!

To my family – Mike and Lisa,
Mackenzie, Sam, Josh and Lance
– You are the blessings that I count every day.

By failing to prepare,
You are preparing to fail.
– *Benjamin Franklin*

Your people are more important than your stuff!
- *Jean Long Manteufel*

Acknowledgments

Introduction

1	Make yourself at home – at any age	1
2	Music connects for those living with dementia	5
3	Collectibles are memories that take up lots of space	9
4	How to split Mom's estate fairly among the children	13
5	Moments of grief: Be careful with emotional decisions	17
6	Do homework regarding a parent's ability to drive	21
7	When is the right time to leave your house?	25
8	Wait 8: Hold off on social media to announce sad news	29
9	Some decisions can be tough	33
10	Veterans must seek out individual benefits	37
11	Consider the 80/20 rule when it's time to downsize	41
12	Let Dad know that you will always have his back	45
13	Connecting through human touch	49
14	Leaving long-time home can be difficult	53
15	Document belongings in case of theft	57
16	Tips for visitin parents in long-term care facilities	61
17	Stay in tune with seniors as they prepare to move	65
18	T.H.A.N.K.S. for helping with end of life issues	69
19	Expand your interactions to stay connected	73
20	Take a swing at cleaning out the basement	77

21	Generations come together to learn together	81
22	Stay organized: Some tips for seniors on move	85
23	Caregiving impacts you at work	89
24	Let's make Box-It Day a thing on December 26	93
25	Organize photos now to help 'generation gap' later	97
26	Someone to watch over me	101
27	Even in volunteer work, change can be difficult	105
28	Shredding old papers is part of protecting yourself	109
29	Seeing primary doctor is important as you age	113
30	Falls are preventable with a little bit of education	117
31	Don't be afraid to dig into your closet	121
32	Lots to be thankful for, even as we age	125
33	Clearing out parents' home comes with big emotions	129
34	Educate aging parents about charity scams	133
35	Sort as you decorate for the seasons	137
36	Program welcomes those with dementia	141
37	The New Year is a time for change… or is it?	145
38	Great gift ideas for your aging parents, grandparents	149
39	Consider bits of your history to pass on	153
40	Caring for aging senior? Here's where to find help	157
41	Collections often have great value… but not financial	161
42	Benefits available to wartime vets	165
43	Senior centers have "everything A-Z"	169

44	Bit by painful bit, Alzheimer's stole from us	173
45	Give the gift of an old memory	177
46	Thirty minutes that changed a life forever	181
47	Readers are invited to share ideas on loneliness	185
48	Readers seek ways to overcome loneliness	189
49	Readers share ideas on overcoming loneliness	193
50	A clean attic is a gift for the whole family	197
51	Uncertainty of a new home can be daunting	201
52	Let's make a deal	205
53	Game plan needed as kids divide up possessions	209
54	A handy list for when a loved one passes away	213
55	Who are columns about? This time, it is Mom	217
56	Bloom where you're planted	221
57	Transitions trivia: Can you make the right call?	225

About the Author   229

Acknowledgments

It wouldn't be possible for me to do all of the fun things I do if it weren't for the supportive people that fill my life.

There is my fantastic family, headed up by my super mom, Gladie Long. Thanks, Mom, for being my biggest champion. Also, thanks for letting me put you on the cover and for your drawings. I know you love me; I love you more!

At work, there are ladies who support me, so that I can do my many projects. Thank you, Denise Wichman for keeping the show running smoothly. Denise, you rock! Thanks also to Jennifer Van Rossum. I really couldn't have done this book without your help. Thank you for not swearing at your computer as loudly as you would like to.

Keith Zentner, thank you for always promptly reviewing my columns. You really know your grammar and punctuation. It is just a bonus that I get to jerk your chain so often.

My sister, Laura Long Muinde, helps me in more ways than she can know. She is a great editor, my friend, my matron-of-honor forty years ago, and for the last several years, she has been my assistant at Long's Senior Transitions. That officially makes her my "assister"! Thanks, Laura.

I have another family; my Kiwanis family. Through Kiwanis, I receive the gift of giving to others. Would you like to check out Kiwanis? Let me know. I love to share.

Introduction

There comes a time when it all gets to be too much to handle; when we get overwhelmed.

We are overwhelmed with taking care of our beloved one; overwhelmed with keeping up the house; overwhelmed with the loss of our physical abilities; overwhelmed with what to do with all of the treasures we have collected over the years; just plain overwhelmed.

For almost a decade, I've been writing a column encouraging folks to keep moving forward in life, use the resources available so you can manage change early and while you are able to be in charge rather than wait until you are overwhelmed.

Actually, that is a word I hear 4-5 times a week, usually while talking to someone who is getting ready to make a transition. As they are trying to describe what is going on in their life – with either their loss of ability to do things themselves or with health challenges they are having, out pops that word; they let out a big sigh and simply say, "I'm overwhelmed."

My goal is to get us all thinking, talking and planning. Whittle away at your tasks now, bit by bit. Don't wait until those tasks become an obstacle to joyful living. Together, we can do this!

1   Make yourself at home – at any age

It is that time of the year. As they are heading off to college, freshmen students are starting a new adventure in their lives. It is exciting. It is scary. It is a big step. Nothing back at home will be the same again. Part of the journey is planning what fits into that dorm room.

Students and their parents are out shopping for just the right stuff. Space in the new room is limited. It is all about selecting items that are practical and functional.

Just as important as function is personality. Each student wants their room to reflect their style. It is their opportunity to express themselves.

If you Google "how to decorate a dorm room", you will find almost all the same suggestions as when you Google "how to decorate a senior's assisted living apartment".

One of the big differences is that seniors already have a whole house full of things from which they can choose. Their challenge is narrowing it down to the precious few.

The staff at the senior communities doesn't mind at all if you decorate the new room. They encourage it. The more comfortable and home-like the room is, the more their new resident will feel welcome.

Start with the functional furniture. Get the size of the room and determine what will fit. Factor in windows and doors. If Mom normally gets out of bed on the left side to go to the bathroom, then try to set up her new bed that way. Consider the size of the bed. For one person, a queen size bed takes up a lot of space in a small room.

Next is storage. "Shop" around the house for furniture that fits. Often the guest bedroom has smaller dressers than the big master suite. Curio cabinets are great. They are nice for displaying knick-knacks.

Try to duplicate her home environment. If Mom is accustomed to having a nightstand and lamp next to her bed, try to do the same. Take her favorite chair for watching TV and don't forget a couple of smaller chairs for guests.

This isn't about creating "house beautiful" and worrying about what matches. Instead, it is about making a "home beautiful" and recreating a place that is warm, inviting and comfortable to her.

You'll want her favorite throw pillows, her family pictures. Give her room color and texture. Sheets, pillows and her blanket that are familiar are appreciated. Special mementos are a must. Ask her to help with choices.

Not everything has to be decided on the first day. You want to get her settled in but can add (or subtract) more items later. Perhaps you can store totes of seasonal decorations so you can change things out for her once in a while.

The goal is to take a room that is institutional, plain and boring, and turn it into something that makes the best use of space and, most importantly, reflects the life of the resident – whether that resident is 19 or 90.

2   Music connects for those living with dementia

Dear Jean:

Mom has dementia and lives in a memory care place. Something that frustrates me when I go visit is the music they play on the sound-system.

It is typical to hear songs that are jarring to the peace. Recently, I heard the Rolling Stones, followed by Rod Stewart singing Hot Legs. Those songs are alright in certain settings, but Mom (and her generation) hated them when we played them in high school. They aren't soothing to her. I have asked the aide to change it. She said they don't have a choice, "it is what is on the radio".

There has also been modern country music playing on the CD player in the dining room.

Several times, the wife of one of the residents asked if she could play her own CD's for the 12 residents while they are dining. One aide continuously says no. I think the staff just plays the music that they like. It really bugs me.

My sister says I should leave them alone, that it isn't a battle worth fighting, but I know that the right music can be relaxing to Mom. What can I do?

Answer:

The experts in dementia care agree with you. Music has been found to make a huge difference to folks with dementia. To take a quote from Alzheimers.net: "Overall, care facilities report that residents are happier, more engaged, and much calmer with the use of music therapy. They note that staff members are able to create more meaningful relationships with patients, spending less time dealing with behavioral issues. Perhaps most encouraging, some facilities are actually seeing a reduction in the need for psychotropic drugs, which carry with them a set of problems all their own."

The right music can decrease anxiety, help calm the environment and evoke warm memories. Isn't that what "memory care" is all about?

Although the community is where the staff works, it is the residents' home. The music is for the residents. Instead of confronting the aides (who also appear to appreciate music) talk to the director. Be an advocate. Share the benefits that the right music can bring to all of their residents, explain your challenges and ask him/her to get involved. You can even offer to help find appropriate music based on whatever the sound system uses.

In your mom's room you can set up an iPod and speakers or whatever works for you. Put together your own playlist of her favorites. You will be amazed at how much pleasure it will bring her.

Music is personal. Pick the songs she remembers, where the words jump right into her head. Popular tunes might include: "Somewhere Over the Rainbow," "You are My Sunshine," "Singing in the Rain," "Amazing Grace," "America the Beautiful," "I Left My Heart in San Francisco." I'll bet you are humming already.

In his song, I Believe in Music, B.J. Thomas sings: "Music is the universal language and love is the key." It seems to be especially fitting for people with memory loss.

3 Collectibles are memories that take up lots of space

Look at me! I'm a pretty pink dish. I was born during the Great Depression; coming into your life in 1932, when you were just a babe.

The Depression was a bleak time for your mother. Dad had to find work where he could. A plumber by trade, maybe he fixed a sink one month, or maybe a pipe. His customers could hardly pay. He would bring home the few dollars and turn them over to your mom. She ran the household on a pittance.

Four children at home meant that every penny had to stretch. One day, she opened a box of oatmeal and found me! It put a smile on her face that was normally strained from hardship. Quaker Oats had started putting glass dishes in with their oats. Other businesses followed.

Your mom's collection began, and then she added to it. When Dad went to the gas station, they would reward him with a glass cup. (Personally, I think I helped keep the economy moving during the 1930s.)

Your mom always kept her pink glass in a place of honor. She had worked so hard to scrimp and save for us, sometimes sneaking behind Dad's back to buy an extra piece that she coveted.

When she passed away in the 1970s, I went home with you. Oh, happy days. Looking at me filled you with nostalgia. I reminded you of your mom and your childhood, of harder times and of rays of sunshine.

You started adding to her collection. Going to auctions on the weekends became a great pastime for you, seeking out more Depression glass. You added greens, and yellows, carnival glass and pretty plates. I'll admit I felt a bit jealous. I didn't feel special anymore, just one of many.

You weren't alone in your pursuit. Your peers joined in. Our values rose. When you went on vacation, you would scour antique stores. The fun was in the hunt. You bought a china cabinet to display us in. How pretty we looked with the lights dancing off of our multi-colors. We made you smile.

Now you have lots of Depression glass and various other treasures that you enjoyed collecting, like Hummels, figurines and plates.

The time has come to reduce your collections down to a precious few. By sheer volume, we've lost our uniqueness. Now our value isn't in dollars, it is in your memories.

Your other collectables remind you of the hunt, but I am delightful because I remind you of your mom. You've asked your kids if they'll take some of us. They took a piece or two, but they didn't grow up during the Depression. They don't have your memories, nor do your grandchildren.

Take me! Take me! We had fun, didn't we?

So, I go with you to your new home. I am honored to remain part of your life. Someday, perhaps your granddaughter will look at me, remembering you, her sweet grandma and your stories; she will smile and want me after all.

4   How to split Mom's estate fairly among the children

Dear Jean: Mom moved into assisted living. She asked me to help divide the items in our family home and get it cleared-out for selling. I have a brother and two sisters. It has really been stressful for Mom.

There is nothing of great dollar value, but there are things of great emotional value, to some. One sister has started asking Mom for things already and has taken her children there. How do I do it in a fair way?

Answer:

This is a team activity; every team needs a leader and a goal.

 Be a leader. Ask the family to stop. No one takes anything until everyone is together. You are all on your honor.

Then, decide what your goals are. (More on suggested goals in a minute.)

Pick the soonest date when all five of you can be there together. Make it a priority, for Mom's sake.

Prepare ahead:

- Just the four children and Mom; no spouses nor grandchildren.
- Write up and share a game-plan.
- Pick legacy items - items so special that they shouldn't leave the family, even if they are worth money. Examples might be: grandma's sterling silverware, great-grandpa's shaving mug... There are four of you. Pick four, eight, twelve... each receives the same number of legacy items.
  - Set a goal for when the house is to be emptied.

  - Put up signs:
  - "Legacy items are never to be sold. If you don't want them later, they should be gifted back to the family."
- "Except for the legacy items, any gift belongs to the person who picks it. They can keep it, sell it, donate it or pass it along."
- "Not included." (Do appliances stay with the house? Is the boat to be sold?)
- "On your turn, pick any item you want – house, yard, basement."

- "Any disagreement will be settled by a show of hands." (Don't make Mom settle agreements, but her word is final.)
- Sets can stay together. The matching dining room is a set. The Lazy-boy and TV is not.

Day of gathering:

- Give each child a notepad, pen, tape and a marker.
- Someone keeps a list of the order to follow and who picks what. Mom might find it helpful later.
- Have snack trays and soda.
- Keep it moving - get done in one day.

Ready, set, go!

- Set the tone by holding hands in a circle and restate the goals – perhaps: "The first goal is to keep family harmony. The second goal is to pick items in the house until we each feel we are finished. The third goal is to keep family harmony. The fourth goal is to get the house cleared-out, so it can be sold. The fifth goal is to keep family harmony."
- Give them ½ hour to go around the house and make their wish-list.
- Throw names in a bowl and pick to see who goes first.
- Start with divvying-up the legacy items.
- Then do all other items.
- When they pick, they either put the item in their pile or put their name on it.

Have fun! Share memories!

Note to readers: After this column, I received several notes suggesting that the order be rotated, moving the one who picked last the opportunity to pick first on the next round.

i.e: 1,2,3,4   4,1,2,3   3,4,1,2   2,3,4,1   1,2,3,4 …

5   Moments of grief: Be careful with emotional decisions

"She is dead to me." The angry voice came from a sixtyish man across the ICU waiting room that I was in.

It is a very private, yet public place. There can be intense family conversations going on nearby, while you are worrying about your own special person.

He was talking to a woman, maybe his wife. His 90-year-old mother was in surgery and declining. He was talking about his niece. "She is dead to me." He repeated. "Ma has been in the hospital for three weeks. Jenny refuses to visit her own grandma."

I reflected back to when I was 18 and my Grandma Hyacinth was in the hospital for a month. I never went to see her. Not once. Mom implored me to go see Grandma: "She misses you. Please go visit her."

Nope. I was too busy. Too wrapped up in my own life. Too scared. I didn't want to see Grandma fading. Denial. Creeped out. Self-centered.

That is part of the journey. Learning. Maturing.

People handle death and dying in many ways. It is natural to feel guilt, denial, anger and frustration.

It sounded like that man was handling it by lashing out.

I wondered if his mother was like mine. Mom built our family on the foundation of "If you don't have something nice to say, don't say anything at all."

With Mom's eight children, she reinforced it with: "Get along," "Don't say 'hate'," "Take your sister with you" and "Get over it." We simply weren't allowed to dislike our brothers and sisters.

Listening to that man's pain, I wanted to give him a hug and explain the destruction he could wield with the blow of that momentary decision.

When you decide to cut someone off, it affects the whole family.

At the eventual funeral, when they should be celebrating his mother's life, would he instead be making sure that everyone knows what a horrible person his niece is? And when he does that, won't his sister, the niece's mother, have to take a stand, further tearing down what his mom had built?

Months down the road, perhaps at a wedding, would he insist that if the niece is going to be there, he won't go, then want others to side with him?

I wanted to tell him that he could dislike her actions, but to get over it. Just be civil. If you don't have anything nice to say, don't say anything at all.

Being part of a family means responsibility. Trust me. Did I mention there are eight kids in our family? Sometimes we get on each other's nerves. Sometimes we have to work on it. But it is worth it. We are family.

The death of someone we love is a very difficult time. Celebrate their memory by pulling the family together, not tearing it apart.

I deeply regret not visiting Grandma when she was failing. I can't change that. I hope he did not end up doing something he can't change.

6   Do homework regarding a parent's ability to drive safely

Dear Jean: My mom is 79 and I think she is too old to drive. My brother said she is fine, and I should leave her alone. We argue about it often. Who is right?

Answer: Age alone is not a reason for a person to stop driving. The real question is whether your mom can drive safely.

To answer that, I chatted with Nicholas Jarmusz, Director of Public Affairs at AAA Wisconsin. He said that taking away a parent's right to drive can be traumatic. You want to avoid an intervention. If not handled well, it may cause a rift within families and between generations.

Jarmusz said: "It is a unique situation for each driver. It should be a unique conversation for each family."

His advice is to get parents on board and encourage them to determine for themselves if and when they stop driving. "Start talking about it early. Now. Not after the crash."

AAA has an excellent website that really helps with this discussion. Find it at www.seniordriving.AAA.com The site's central goal "is to help you drive as long as safely possible."

They say "age should never be used as the sole indicator of driving ability…. However, it is not uncommon for some of the skills necessary for safe driving – such as vision, reflexes, flexibility, and hearing – to begin to deteriorate as we age."

Keeping that in mind, they have some great tools to help you and your mom out.

Some of the topics on their website are:

- Improve Your Driving Skills
- Maintain Mobility & Independence

And for family and friends they have:

- Conversations About Driving
- Know When to Be Concerned

They also have a section called "Evaluate Your Driving Ability". It is a self-rating test. By answering 15 questions, it measures strengths and weaknesses; it then shares ideas about how to improve your driving. Your mom can take it and grade it herself.

By your parent taking the test once a year, as he or she notices changes, they can modify habits to keep themselves and others safe. By the way, you should take it too. I did.

Jarmusz explained some of the ways you can adjust your driving as you experience changes.

You may decide to start limiting when and where you drive, such as no longer driving at night because it is harder to see; avoiding driving during rush hour to avoid the pressure; and no longer driving more than X miles from home.

What's next? Because you know that someday you will be a retired driver, start looking now for options for getting around. Practice them so you get comfortable with alternatives. It doesn't have to be a sudden change. Start carpooling to your lunches, check out local transit options and call your local senior center for ideas.

Jarmusz ended with: "Like teen driving, keys represent freedom. To teens it is getting freedom. Now, we aren't giving up freedom, but rather looking for new ways to get around."

7   When is the right time to leave your house?

Dear Jean,

It always sounds like you want people to move out of their house. I totally disagree. It is their choice. They should stay in their homes as long as they want. Why do you do that?

Answer:

Indeed, I often strongly encourage people to make a move from their house. That isn't necessarily because I consider it to be the best choice. Let me explain.

To me, the best option is for folks to be safe, comfortable and enjoying their life, wherever it is that makes that happen.

People contact me for one of two reasons; they are either planners, or they are delayers, who are now facing a crisis.

Planners may be remodeling their current home to meet future needs, wearing a "push-button for help" pendant, hiring someone to maintain the yard, installing safety features and allowing a service to come in to do cleaning and caregiving.

Planning ahead may also be deciding that the family house has outgrown their needs. They are moving to a place that they enjoy, where friends are around and where there is a continuum of care, so that when eventually more assistance is needed, it is readily available.

Delayers, on the other hand, don't want to think about what might happen. If you ask them what their intentions are, they firmly reply "I'm staying in my house until I die".

In a perfect world, we would like to remain together in our beloved home, where we raised our growing family. It would never become a burden to maintain. We would live to be 90+ years old; then die peacefully in our sleep, together. After the memorial service (where the kids agree on everything), the heirs would gather at the house and peacefully divide up the contents.

This is not sarcasm. It is really what many folks dream will happen.

Look around at your friends. Is this reality?

So, I ask, if you don't talk now about the future, what will you do when there is a calamity and you are forced to make a change?

The answer I hear most is: "We'll deal with that when it happens."

Let's think about that. What might be occurring in your life that would require you to leave your home unprepared and unwillingly? Generally, the answer is failing health or death of a spouse. During that trauma, it is not the time to start selecting a new place to move and dealing with all the challenges that comes with the transition.

Can we agree that the day will come when you shouldn't be driving anymore? What then?

Can we agree that you or your spouse may someday have a stroke or be diagnosed with cancer, dementia or heart disease? What then?

Waiting leaves families struggling and puts more stress on someone who is already vulnerable.

You say that people should decide where to live, so do I. We just disagree on when. I want people to make a plan, so the future is their choice and they aren't forced into a situation with no good choices.

If you want to stay in your home, now is the time to take steps to make that happen.

If you really don't want to do all of that work later, at a time when you are under stress, please start now to consider what your next step will be.

8   Wait 8: Hold off on social media to announce sad news

What is sadder than losing your dad? Answer: Learning about it on Facebook before your sister even has a chance to call you.

It happened again to a friend of mine. It is going to be hard for her to get over it. It was unintentional, but what a cruel way to hear bad news about a loved one.

If someone special passed away an hour ago, there hasn't been enough time to call the whole family. Twitter can wait. Before you hit "send"; stop and think. A brother might be driving and not checking his phone. A sister might be at work and doesn't even look at her phone until lunch time. Wait.

Sure, you want to be the one to share the news with the world. Yes, you want your friends to know you are in pain. Wait a bit.

48 hours? 24 hours? Can we at least agree to wait 8 hours? Please.

If you were just told of someone's death, wait 8. Wait just 8 hours after they have died to post or tweet. Wait 8.

Have you ever noticed in the media that they don't tell you the name of someone who died "pending notification of next-of-kin"? That is because the family needs a little time to contact all the really important people who should know, before the rest of the world is told. It is a courtesy. It is compassionate. It is the right thing to do.

Make a family agreement with all the generations to "wait 8". Agree now, before someone else's heart is crushed.

There is a second thing about social media that we should discuss.

Have you noticed that we all don't use the same way to communicate? Everyone has their favorite way to be contacted and they also have ways they never, ever use.

My daughter, a nurse, hardly ever answers her phone. Heaven forbid, I send her an email. She won't check it for a week. If I want something, it is "Text me, Mom".

For my husband, it is the phone only, and don't leave a voicemail. He doesn't know how to listen to it. Just keep calling until you get him. He turns it off when driving (a good thing).

My pal, Mike, started sending me messages through Facebook. The first time I read a note from him, it was five weeks old. I don't use Facebook for messaging.

Do not assume everyone uses the same method that you do.

I've texted information to someone, only to find out later that their phone doesn't accept texts.

My mom doesn't check email every day. It isn't her key form of communication. One of her cousins died and the news was sent by email. Mom didn't see it until a week after the funeral. She would have wanted to go to her cousin's funeral. It hurt.

When you have a very important message, make sure that it is received by the person it really matters to and "wait 8" for the rest of the world.

9   Some decisions can be tough

Did you ever read something that really hit home with you? This week, I did.

Here it is: "I am not a second-guesser. I believe you make decisions with the best of intentions, with the best information you can find, with the best awareness of your circumstances, and you live with the consequences." It was in a blog by Dan Flannery, talking about his relationship with his dad. (More about Flannery in a moment.)

It struck me because it reflects my thoughts on how we might handle choices about our parents as they are aging.

Sometimes, we don't agree with their choices.

Elizabeth's children listened when she insisted that she didn't want to move from her house - ever. When her health seriously declined, they still tried to make her wish happen, as best as they could. They tried to convince her to let them hire help. She refused to have strangers in her house. The kids did everything they could to keep her home, including taking shifts staying with her.

Sometimes they just couldn't handle the load, so they checked her in to nursing home for respite; maybe just for a weekend. She was upset with them every time they did. They lived with that consequence, because they really didn't have a choice. They wanted to help her, but also needed to help themselves survive.

When she passed away, Elizabeth's family knew they had done everything with the best of intentions. They made the best choices they could, under the circumstances. They didn't second-guess their decisions.

In contrast, Amanda's parents lived two hours away from both Amanda and her brother, Mark. Her parents insisted that they wanted to stay independent. Over time, Amanda and her brother grew very concerned about their parents' safety. Dad was diagnosed with Parkinson's disease. Mom insisted that she could take care of him. Eventually, she couldn't.

Amanda and her brother talked it over. They knew Mom and Dad wouldn't leave their house willingly.

Amanda and Mark looked for an assisted-living home for their parents. The brother and sister went to their parents' house together, on a Saturday and moved them. No discussion.

Three years later, Dad still complains about it, but he and Mom are now well settled in. They have help and friends.

Amanda and Mark had their parent's best interest in mind. They made the best choice they could, under the circumstances. They did not second-guess their decision.

Who was right? Maybe they both are. As Flannery said, we have to "make decisions with the best of intentions, with the best information you can find, with the best awareness of your circumstances, and you live with the consequences."

So, back to Dan Flannery. You remember Dan? He worked at the Post Crescent for almost 30 years, culminating his career there as Executive Editor. He was a great storyteller. Still is. Now he writes a blog called The Sunday Column. You can find it, and subscribe to it, at www.DanLFlannery.com

10   Veterans must seek out individual benefits

Veterans, do you wonder what benefits are out there for you and how you can get them? Perhaps you have tried to find out, but it was all so complicated.

Wouldn't it be nice if there was someone out there who would look up benefits specifically for you; what benefits you earned based on your DD214? While you're at it, let's wish they would explain how to apply for your earned benefits; heck, let's even wish that they would help fill out the forms. Finally, wouldn't it be great if this help was free?

Meet your county Veterans Service Office.

I chatted with David Holst, Outagamie County Veterans Service Officer. The sign jokingly put on his door by his staff says "One-Stop Shop". That is his goal.

He explained that many veterans are unaware of what services are available to them. He said it is "like wordsmithing: The right terms and the right forms in the right order trigger benefits, otherwise it doesn't happen." Here is someone in your corner who speaks the language.

He said people talk with their friends and someone says, "I qualify for this benefit, you should get it, too." It doesn't work like that.

Your benefits are based on your service alone; everybody is as unique as a snowflake. You could have identical twins go into the exact same unit and come out with different benefits.

Holst encourages you to let Veterans Services help. "Our services are free. We even help you fill out the paperwork and we'll send it in if you want. We'll make a copy for you. I'll even be your secretary, if you need me. The forms can be hard to understand. You provide us with the information, and we'll put it on your form. You verify and sign it. It is your claim, we are here to help you."

Don't confuse your county Veterans Service Office with the federal Veteran's Administration (VA). "We are not employed by the VA." Holst explained. "We are accredited with the VA and we work with the VA, but we do not work for the VA. We are employed by you, the taxpayers of this county."

There is a Veterans Service office in each county of Wisconsin.

The VA doesn't come looking for you to give you benefits. Even if you go to the VA clinic on a regular basis, you won't necessarily know what benefits are available to you.

If you go to your Veterans Service Office, they will help you. It is what they do.

Call your County Veterans Service Office and make an appointment to do a benefits review. It only takes one hour. They will explain all the benefits that you have earned: health care, education, pension, compensation... there are many types of benefits. Once you have your list, you can decide if you want to pursue them. Maybe you don't need them now, but down the road you may want to explore them.

Another note: Veterans Day is a time to honor our veterans. Tell your children and grandchildren about a veteran in your family and teach them to say thank you.

11 Consider the 80/20 rule when it's time to downsize

The first time I heard of the Pareto Principle, it was from an Appleton police detective. He used the expression when explaining that 80 percent of the crimes were committed by 20 percent of the people.   It sounded right.

The Pareto Principle is also known as the 80/20 rule; that approximately 80 percent of the results come from 20 percent of the effort.

Let's see if it makes sense for you. Do you think 80 percent of a teacher's time is taken by 20 percent of their students? You folks in sales, does 80 percent of your income result from 20 percent of your customers? Do you spend 80 percent of your time with 20 percent of your friends? Even, when you read your newspaper, do you spend 80 percent of the time reading 20 percent of it? I know I do.

The Pareto Principle is a great concept for folks when they are moving to a senior community.

Once our kids have moved out, we spend 80 percent of our life in 20 percent of our house. Right? We have a well-worn path between the kitchen, bedroom, bathroom and the living room (or whatever you call the room that your recliner, TV and remote are in).

The other 80 percent of your house probably isn't even walked into most of the time. Just thinking about clearing out all those areas can be exhausting. So, don't!

Do you spend 80 percent of your time in 20 percent of your clothes? Consider what you are wearing right now. I'll bet you wear it often, because it is comfortable.

So, here is the lesson for downsizers: Concentrate on the relevant 20 percent. Stop stressing on the 80 percent that is just stuff. It will burn 80 percent of your energy dealing with it. Stop, stop, stop.

Senior communities do a wonderful job of creating the perfect space for you, as you need less square footage and have less desire to maintain it.

In the privacy of your apartment, you have those important areas that you already spend 80 percent of your time; the kitchen, bedroom, bathroom and living room.

When you start planning to move, you want to identify that crucial 20 percent of the items that you enjoy 80 percent of your time. Of course, the 20 percent that is important to you isn't the same as someone else's.

Pick out the things that you love and enjoy and use; that fulfill your needs.

A hint for clearing out that closet: If there is still a price tag on it, then it never was part of your key 20 percent.

If you follow the Pareto Principle when you are moving, you might be quite surprised that you will hardly miss the 80 percent, the stuff that is just stuff. It is freeing.

Repeatedly, when we have moved folks to a senior community, they are surprised by how comfortable they are with less, often saying that they don't miss all that stuff.

I am hoping that, by now, 80 percent of you are smiling, nodding your head and thinking, "Jean sure makes a good point."

12   Let Dad know that you will always have his back

Dear Jean,

Father's Day is coming up. I don't know what to get for Dad. He has lost so much of his memory. At times, he doesn't even know me. Why bother?

Dad isn't the same person he used to be. Sometimes he thinks I am his younger brother, Bill, who died in Korea. It hurts.

For the most part, Mom now takes care of the house. She says she wants to do it while she can. Fortunately, Dad is still mostly able to care for himself. My sister found someone to do their yard work, and she takes them to their doctor visits.

I help by paying their bills. I stay with Dad for a couple of hours every week so Mom can get out of the house. We just sit, and he talks about things that happened 70 years ago. I want to go out for dinner or a game or something, but he just wants to stay in.

Two years ago, the neighbors called me because his driving was so unsafe. I eventually had to get him to stop driving. Mom and my sister agreed that it was the right thing to do, but I felt awful.

I feel like a mean child.

Answer:

Oh my. Don't you see it? You are giving him the best Father's Day gift of all. You and your sister have his back.

Let's consider the letter you would have written ten years ago, if you had known the future.

"Dear Dad,

For Father's Day, Sis and I want you to know that we'll always be there for you and for Mom. And we'll do it together.

When the day comes that you can no longer drive safely, we'll make sure that you won't hurt yourself or anyone else. We'll be strong when you can't be.

Your bills will still be paid on time and that your finances will be well protected.

I'll listen to your stories knowing that it gives you comfort to relive memories. Don't worry that you'll repeat yourself or that you won't remember things anymore. It's OK. I'll be there for you.

Sometimes you tell me that I remind you of Uncle Bill. He's obviously somebody you miss. I'm glad you see him in me.

As your energy runs down, I'll keep in mind that just being there means so much. Even if you don't remember me, I'll make sure you feel my love through companionship, a touch, my time.

Dad, we'll stand by you. You can lean on us. We'll be there for you and Mom, always. You will never have to worry about what happens when you are unable to take care of things yourself. We've got your back.

I'll make mistakes. I'll be impatient. But I'll do my best.

And Dad, as you are reaching the end of your journey through life, we'll still be there and do our best to make sure you aren't alone.

Dad I love you, and I want you to know that we've got your back. Happy Father's Day."

13   Connecting through human touch

Recently, I met an engaging gal. She was shyly giving a presentation to the Fox Valley Senior Resource Network. Wendy Wilson is a licensed massage therapist and owner of Integrative Massage & Bodyworks.

She wasn't comfortable with public speaking and even quipped that most people she addresses are laying face-down, while she talks to the back of their head.

Wilson shared her passion for helping seniors through massage: "A well-done massage can be an incredibly relaxing experience. It washes away the muscle aches of a long day. We assume that our aging population doesn't have the same tensions as the young, but that isn't true. They face a wide variety of emotional and physical problems, ranging from loneliness and depression, to an aging body that carries the effects of a lifetime of hard work.   There is arthritis, degenerative disease, numerous surgeries and Alzheimer's."

Wilson started her stories with "I'd like you to meet June. She is 81 years old and has been in a nursing facility for many years."

"June's caregivers had warned me of a belligerent, violent resident who would throw glasses of water at anyone who entered her room. They were right.

"My first meeting with June left me wet and a little shaken. But I stayed 15 minutes with her, mostly in silence, occasionally talking about the fat squirrel outside her window. Through the course of conversation, I would touch her hand, her elbow or her shoulder. I asked about her hands and commented how strong they were.

"She lived in the past, telling me how milking the cows that morning had made her hands hurt or how carrying the feed bags made her shoulders ache.

"Over the next six weeks, we became farm-hands together. I was able to enter her room without getting doused with water and actually would be greeted with a smile. Her caregivers noticed a huge change too. June was no longer combative and was sleeping much better - because someone gave her some caring touch."

Wilson continued, "Nellie is an 82-year-old grandma who drives to Madison every month to watch her grandchildren, goes to Zumba at the Y and crochets washcloths for gifts. She thinks I am an angel, relieving her pain, and reducing her stress and anxiety.

"Wayne is a hospice patient, who loves the touch therapy and wants me to keep coming."

Hearing the soft rhythm of Wilson's voice as she told her stories was relaxing.

She explained that, "Massage has many benefits. When using proper bodywork techniques, it is almost impossible to harm clients." Smiling she added, "That sounds much more attractive than the warning labels on all those medications."

A typical massage for an elder is 30 minutes. Focus can be on hands and feet to facilitate circulation and relieve pain, or a back rub or a full body massage.

While massage decreases stiffness and reduces inflammation, it also enhances circulation, combats depression, reduces pain, increases mobility, decreases blood pressure and provides comfort - especially to touch-deprived clients.

And it just feels good.

14   Leaving long-time home can be difficult

Do you remember your first day of school?

My grandson, Josh, is getting ready to start first grade this week, which reminded me of my first day at St. Mary's Grade School. It was so long ago, and I barely recall the details, but I still remember the feelings.

Before that, like many of my generation, I just played at home with my brothers and sisters, and with the neighbor kids. My world was pretty small.

Starting school was a big deal. Mom took me shopping for a new school uniform, shoes, socks and blouses, even a matching headband. It was cool picking my very own box of crayons and No. 2 pencils. I wouldn't have to share those crayons with my sisters. How grown-up I was.

Although I was excited about the new things, I was also nervous about what I was getting into. Everything at home was comfortable. Fear of the unknown causes lots of anxiety.

It was pretty overwhelming; new surroundings and new kids to meet. Would they like me? Would I fit in? I had butterflies.

I told Mom that I wanted to stay home. Couldn't things just stay the way they were?

"You can do this." I remember her saying.

Then, my world changed anyway.

Mom took me to school and into the gym where all the classes were gathering. I remember gripping her hand tightly, as we walked over to where the first graders were lined up. Then she gently squeezed my hand and walked away.

I didn't know a soul in sight. The butterflies were pounding their wings.

Shyly, I spoke to the girl next to me. "Hi."

"Hi." She timidly relied.

"My name is Jean," I said. "What's yours?"

"Jean." She answered back. Surely, she was teasing me. It ended up we both had the same name. That was a new one on me. We started laughing, and my world lightened up a little bit.

Before long, I was enjoying school, my classmates and all of the new activities.

Starting in school is a milestone in our life.

Another milestone is the day we leave the house we have been in for decades, and we move to a senior community. It is stressful leaving a place that is comfortable and familiar.

As you are preparing to move to a new home, think back to those feelings of starting school, and use them to your advantage.

Recognize that making this transition is emotional. It is a big change, and change causes stress. It is stepping away from what is comfortable. It is OK to feel overwhelmed. It means you are normal.

Are you gripping tightly to what is familiar? Let loose a little.

Stay positive. Get support from your family and friends. Avoid those Negative Nellies.

And, when you meet someone, say "Hi", and introduce yourself. They may well be feeling as hesitant as you do. Before you know it, you might both be laughing and enjoying new friendships.

You can do this.

15   Document belongings in case of theft

Dear Jean:

We recently had to deal with the possible theft of my mother's jewelry. Between the in-home caregivers, visitors and family, we didn't know who might have taken it. Before we made any accusations, we searched long and hard.

After much worry, fortunately we discovered that nothing was missing. It was merely misplaced by Mom, who has memory issues and keeps moving things.

Some families aren't so lucky. Please offer suggestions on how to handle suspected theft, and also how to catalog valuables, especially items of worth such as art, jewelry and stamp/coin collections.

We don't know what we should have done if the jewelry really had been gone.

Answer:

I'm pleased to know that all ended well. It is great that you did a thorough search before accusing anyone. As you found out, if you had blamed someone, you could have been very wrong.

If a person suspects theft, the first step, which you did, is to hunt through the house, question Mom and quiz the family. Then contact your police department and your insurance company. Remember though, just because you suspect something, doesn't make it so. Nor does it automatically mean you can collect insurance on it.

As explained to me by an insurance adviser, Curt Fritz from Adamino & Associates, unless you have a rider added to your insurance policy, theft is usually limited to a low amount, like $2,500. That is not per item, but for the full loss. To purchase a rider, you need an appraisal, which is where a professional person documents the value.

If your mom has jewelry of very high value, and doesn't use it all the time, encourage her to keep it in a safe-deposit box.

Let's look at how to document the valuables.

Fritz recommended a quick and easy way to catalog your mom's home.

"It doesn't have to be complicated," he said. "Record a video of the house and possessions. It's an invaluable tool to help you remember what you have.

"In just 15 minutes, you can record all the rooms, walk over to items of special value and hold them up to view on the recorder, even turn them over to show their markings. You can talk and provide more detail."

For the police, if things are stolen, having a photo and any significant markings or inscriptions are always helpful in locating the items down the line if pawned or recovered.

If you do the video on your smartphone, record a snippet of each room, then stop and record the next one. Later, you can easily send them to anyone.

It is good to have documentation of what is really in the house. Memories fade, and Mom may not remember that she gave something away months, or years, before.

It helps keep down family squabbles. You've got a record, and all can easily review it.

Be sure to keep a copy somewhere other than the house.

Because it's quicker to do than writing a long list, you could do it this week.

16   Tips for visiting with parents in long-term care facilities

"Jean, this probably is not a good topic, but...can you talk to families about what to do when their parent goes into a long-term care facility? Some think that their family member can never leave again."

That was a note that I received from my sister, Julie Dobberstein, of Fox Valley Guardianship & Payee Services.

Are you kidding, Julie? It is a great topic!

Dobberstein shared suggestions for folks: "Take your mom out to lunch once in a while or to the store so she can pick out her snacks. The community menus don't have her favorite foods."

"Visit. It doesn't have to be long, just stop in." She commented: "I think they don't know what to talk about, so they hate going."

Her advice: "You already know the stories your dad loves to tell; ask him about them like it's your first time hearing them. Remember the good old days."

When you bring treats, do the initial opening of the bags or bottles, to make it easier for them. Open the chip bag and put a clip on it.

Take your dad out for ice cream.

Stop bringing stuffed animals. Instead, bring bananas, shampoo, lotion, soap. Give things that go away - consumables, and not collectibles.

Take them out to get their hair cut/done, pedicures.

After reading Dobberstein's suggestions, I asked an associate for more ideas. Sue Coyle, geriatric care manager at Coyle Care Management and Consulting added:

- Take them out for breakfast.
- Instead of buying a brand-new chair, bedspread or decoration, bring what is familiar to your parent and will look and feel more like home.
- They'll enjoy their own cologne, deodorant, shampoo and toothpaste. These are usually provided, but the constancy of "what I've used for 60 years" feels good.
- Reading materials including magazines and newspapers, if the person is a reader.
- Spiritual materials such as daily devotionals, Bible, Rosary.

- Pictures of family and loved ones. If there are memory impairments, help by labeling who is in the pictures.

I also asked for suggestions from my daughter, Lisa Manteufel, Director of Nursing at Fox River Nursing and Rehab.

Lisa reiterated: "It is helpful to keep things familiar, homey. Make their bed wonderful with a fluffy blanket, their own pillows and sheets."

She agreed with Coyle about the deodorant: "Senior communities use unscented soaps and shampoos, so fragrant personal items are perfect."

- Razors wear out. Take Dad out to select a new one.
- Photo albums are ideal. When you visit, page through and share stories. Reminisce.
- Take Mom shopping at a dollar store.
- If you update clothes and bring some in, go through what they have and take the old ones out. Clutter can be overwhelming in a small environment.
- And no more stuffed animals!"

I laughed when Lisa said that. "I never want stuffed animals," I responded, "Bring me chocolate!"

Looking over these ideas, they are great for just about any senior.

17   Stay in tune with seniors as they prepare to move

From start to finish, a move for a senior can be an overwhelming process. I've put together this ballad to help explain. Let's walk through the journey together. It flows to the tune of "On Top of Old Smokey."

On top of my table, all covered with stuff,
   Are decades of treasures, going through them is tough.

My kids say, "Mom, leave here". I wish they would know,
   To leave this old house, well, it hurts my heart so.

My dear and I lived here, raised our family of four.
   Now I am without him, I hurt to the core.

But time has a way of …moving along.
   I can't keep this house up; I'm just not as strong.

My house has outgrown me; the upkeep's such stress.
   The windows need washing. The garden's a mess.

The times they have changed now; I don't move so quick.
　　Doing laundry in the basement, of that, I am sick!

Old neighbors have left here; I feel so alone.
　　This new place, I am told, will soon feel like home.

Is it true what folks tell me? I will make friends anew.
　　It's hard to make changes, so I hope it is true.

It's so overwhelming. Where do I begin?
　　The list is so long that - I guess I'll jump in.

"Call a Senior Move Manager", my friend tells me true.
　　"She'll help you consider, just what to do."

The gal helps me pick out - the things I should take:
　　The sofa and chairs for - this new home I'll make.

"Take things that are useful, and that you adore.
　　Fewer things will be needed." She says, "Less is more."

From the den I will take a … thing I enjoy,
　　The table my dear made, when he was a boy.

From the bedroom, so special, photos of all,
　　My family mementos, to adorn the new wall.

She says, "Plates and glasses, of each, just take six."
This "Now-sizing" idea, is starting to click.

~ 66 ~

The movers have pulled up. It's now time to go.
    Good-bye to my old house, I will miss you so.

Once I have my things out, the kids can go through
    And take what they wish, they are their memories too.

My gal will then clear out and sell what she can,
    Then get the house ready - to list. That's the plan.

I'm so glad I called her and saved myself grief.
    She made this job easy. What a relief!

I know this adventure - will bring on new things.
    It's time to look forward - to whatever life brings.

A month after moving, my apartment's just so.
    I wish we had done this, a few years ago.

I'm busy with projects. I've met some friends new
    And re-found an old one - from back in high-school.

My new home is lovely, so cheery and bright.
    Don't tell my children, but perhaps they were right.

Consid'ring a new home?   To your house bid adieu.
    Make a transition; you've still got living to do!

18   T.H.A.N.K.S. for helping with end of life issues

Dear Jean: I wonder if it's time to start making plans for when I die.

I always thought my children could do my estate because I don't have much. My brother said the same thing, but since he passed away, his children have been fighting. Now they aren't speaking. It is sad.

What are a few things I can do so this doesn't happen to my family?

Answer: My heart goes out to you. Yes, it is always time to start planning.

"What are just five things we can all do to help our families?" I asked Chris Mares, an attorney who focuses on estate planning.

Mares explained, "It isn't just at death, but even before that. What happens if we are unable to do things for ourselves?" he posed. "What keys can we give our family to help them?"

He talked about providing keys, not in the sense of locking you out of the control. Rather providing a spare key, allowing access when it is needed.

Here is his list, in order of significance. In it, I created a hint to help remember.

Talk. "The most important thing you can do is talk to your family. How can they follow your wishes if you don't tell them what your wishes are?"

Kids, if your parents want to talk, don't put them off, encourage them.

Health Care Power of Attorney. It answers: "Who is going to make my medical decisions if I can't."

"As far as time-sensitive," Mares said, "This is the big one. If something happens, the doctor will look to see who is authorized to make care decisions right now. If you don't have authorization in place, it becomes a long process."

Mares explained: "Many are under the mistaken idea that spouses can automatically make medical decisions for each other. Not anymore."

One place to get a form is from your family doctor. Talk to the person you are asking to make decisions when you can't. Be sure he/she knows your wishes. Make several original copies. Give one to your doctor and to your hospital. Give one to the designated person. Have a second person, and a third.

Answers. Share a list of your financial and legal information. You don't have to tell the amounts, just tell the answers. Where is your bank? Your brokerage accounts? Your lawyer? Your original will (not in the safe deposit box)? Your insurance policies?

Name a Financial Power of Attorney, someone you trust, to help with your finances.

Ask them if they will do it and guide them. Tell the children. If abilities fade, the keys are there to continue paying your bills.

Kind of funeral. "The only thing we know for sure is that we are going to die. Someone has to make decisions about the kind of final arrangements." Mares said.

Go with one of the children to meet with your funeral director. Plan as much or as little as you want.

Share it all with your family. Keep talking.

With your guidance in place, instead of fighting, your children will say **T.H.A.N.K.S.**

19   Expand your interactions to stay connected

Recently, I was visiting an older friend of mine. Emma is 85 years old, in OK health and still living in her house. She broke down in tears, saying that she is so lonely, and she might as well die.

She said her grandchildren don't come to visit much anymore, and that they just don't care. She considered her grandchildren's lack of caring to be the source of her loneliness.

Pulling out a paper and pencil, I drew what I will call Circles of Living. I helped her picture a circle that represented her world twenty years ago. It was surrounded by all the activities she had participated in: work, church, running errands, doing things with her children and grandchildren – all the things that had filled her life.

When she retired, she had happily eliminated one of those circles, "work", but quickly filled that gap with other activities, like joining a retiree group.

As time passed, some of those groups disappeared. (So I crossed them out.) Friends and neighbors moved away. She drove less, until one day she decided not to drive at all - a good thing. Her retiree group got smaller, until she stopped going.

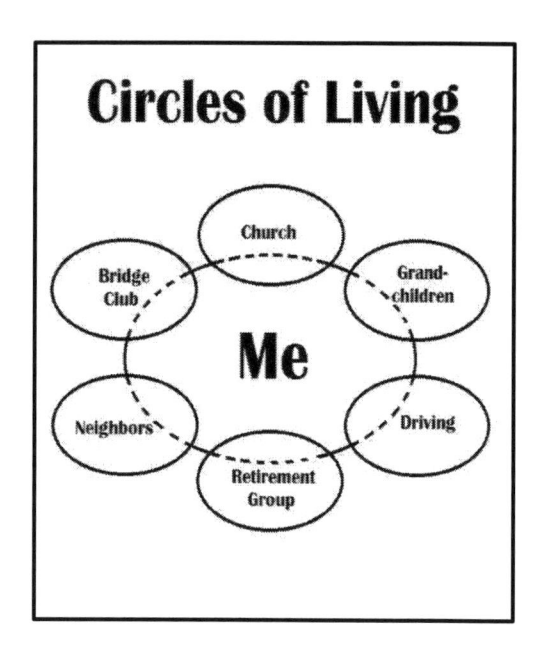

Circles of Living

- Church
- Bridge Club
- Grand-children
- Me
- Neighbors
- Driving
- Retirement Group

When asked further about the grandchildren, she admitted that none of them live within an hour of her, and they all have young children. They call her regularly. One of them visits her every two weeks. It sounded to me like family was the only constant over the years – and that the grandchildren are still there for her, but since she had nothing to fill in the rest of her time, her days were empty.

Do you feel like Emma? Are you lonely?

One day, you wake up and find that your world has gotten so small that it becomes impossible to do anything about it. Are you willing to attack the loneliness?

The key is to add to your circles - as one disappears, find a way to add another.

There is a great pamphlet called "Expand Your Circles – Prevent Isolation and Loneliness As You Age", from the National Association of Area Agencies on Aging (N4A). It includes a self-assessment checklist and gives great ideas on how to refill those circles.

In it, they say: "We need social connection to thrive – no matter our age – but recent research shows that the negative health consequences of chronic isolation and loneliness may be especially harmful for older adults. The good news is that with greater awareness, we can take steps to maintain and strengthen our ties to family and friends, expand our social circles and become more involved in the community around us."

"If you are isolated and lonely now, what can you do?" They advise: "There are lots of opportunities to get engaged in activities you will like, with people you will enjoy."

As you expand your circles, you are also helping those you interact with to expand their circles!

Here is a link to the booklet:
http://www.n4a.org/Files/Isolation%20BrochureFINAL.pdf

20   Take a swing at cleaning out the basement

"Get up! Get outta here! Gone!"

Bob Uecker has a great line. Let's borrow it to clean out a major league opponent, the "Basement". That word brings shivers to even the most strong-hearted folks.

Don't balk. You can go the distance. Not only do we want to win this game; we will sweep the series.

Let's break it down into parts and attack the weaknesses in the "Basement". The batting order is Family Room, Storage Room and, finally, Workroom. You are the pitcher.

Surely, you might admit that 80 percent of the items in the "Basement" haven't been used in 10 years. Or is that 20 years? It's not part of your life anymore.

Our strategy is to use blue painter's tape to tag all the things that we want out, be ruthless in our tagging, and then go to the bullpen to get it gone (kids, grandkids, hire someone).

Leading off is the Family Room. That one might be the shortest stop. For the most part, it is stuff that you no longer use, but you avoided dealing with it. Years ago, it was all on the main floor, and then you found furniture that fit your house better. Rather than cut the stuff, you farmed it out downstairs to keep it, because you "paid good money for it". Recycle those encyclopedias – Strike one. That recliner that broke but was still usable, pitch it. Strike two. Pressboard end tables? Blue tag. Strike three - they're out!

On-deck is the Storage Room. The "Basement" knows you'll have a hard time because you have a long history with this stuff. What about all of that camping gear? You say, "Back in the day, I enjoyed hunting with my brother". "Basement" hits a zinger, reminding you that "It is full of a lot of memories". Don't get run down. If you don't go camping anymore, tag those outdoor supplies. The kids and grandkids might love them. So might the Scouts. It is time to let someone else create new memories with that stuff. Your second room is out.

You give your Dad's duck call an intentional walk. You want to hold onto that memory.

Your final at bat is Workroom. Here is your real nemesis. You look it in the eye. You try to pitch the table saw. "Foul ball," your brain screams. You used to make all kinds of things with it, but you haven't touched it for a long time. Then you remember that your grandson likes to build things, so you summon extra strength from within, and mark it to go. Strike two.

You are getting tired. Put on your rally cap. You can do this!

You eye up the jars of screws, nuts and bolts. "Someday, I might need them," you say. You need an assist, so you call up Habitat Restore. "Sure, we'll be happy to pick up the tools you don't use anymore," they tell you. Relief.

Join the exclusive 40-40 Club. That's 40 things donated, and 40 things gifted. Reward yourself. Go watch the Brewer game. Huzzah!

21 Generations come together to learn together

Kids bring joy to elders. Elders bring joy to kids.

The next obvious step is to get them together.

That is the starting point of a program started by Kim Patterson of Brookdale Appleton Senior Living. Patterson had been an elementary school teacher at St. Pius in Appleton. After 15 years, she switched careers and started at Brookdale, where they emphasize the importance of living the optimum life – fulfilling the six dimensions of well-being: physical, emotional, purposeful, social, spiritual and intellectual (PEPSSI).

Her first thought was "Wow! That is what I learned in my early-childhood training!"

"As a teacher, that was what I loved and knew – the value of connecting the elders with the youth. Both enhance each other's experience," she explained.

She created a plan with the second-grade class at her old school, St. Pius, now renamed St. Francis Xavier Marquette Campus. Throughout the year, they had activities together that covered topics like: Christmas caroling, bringing joy, What does a smile do? and crafting.

She spoke of the delight shared when these generations sit down with each other. "When they are together, it is a happy moment. It brings newness, it brings memories," she said.

The benefit to kids is that they get someone to listen to their stories, someone to share new things with and extra emotional support in their lives. They get to relate with another generation and grow from that experience.

Those are precisely the same benefits that the elders gain from getting together with kids.

Patterson talked about the importance of having a purposeful life. "What is our reason for getting up in the morning? A big part of that is serving others."

She shared Stanford research that found "When older adults contribute to the well-being of youth, it cultivates a sense of purpose and extends both ways."

For the elders, it makes them feel purpose when they are sharing their life-stories; skills they learned in their profession; and even sharing everyday abilities. When they are together, the elders are even teaching the skill of interacting with others; something that has been falling by the wayside with the influx of technology.

For the students, they also feel purpose by being with the elders. They learn the reward of giving of themselves. Patterson talked about the fun the students had when they took a group of elders from Brookdale to their second-grade classroom. Just being in a school again was a grand experience. There were no chalkboards. The kids showed-off their new smart board. What an experience for the seniors. The two generations played interactive games with each other. The elders marveled by it. As the seniors took the smart-pen and wrote their signatures in cursive on the board, the students were amazed by some of their fancy handwriting.

 "Every child needs at least one adult who is irrationally crazy about him or her." - Urie Bronfenbrenner, co-founder of Head Start preschool program.

Patterson is finding a way to bring that child and that adult together.

22   Stay organized: Some tips for seniors on move

Seniors, are you considering a home transition and feeling overwhelmed with all the things to do?

Trying to clean out a house full of a lifetime of items is a daunting task.

First of all, stop working so hard. At 60 years old, there was still time to downsize. Now, at 80, it is too darn much work.

Stop trying to get rid of all the stuff that isn't moving. Don't haul items to charity. Stop cleaning the basement and garage; you aren't going to move any of that anyway, right? It is exhausting.

Instead, concentrate on what is actually moving to your new home. Focus on the life ahead, not on what you are leaving behind.

Get a 5-section notebook, preferably one with pockets. Label the cover: "MY NEXT ADVENTURE!" Keep all of your moving notes in one place.

SECTION 1: WHERE TO MOVE?

Learn the different options for senior living. Check with your Aging and Disability Resource Center for help with what amenities you want and need. Look at your financial resources. When considering a place, ask what services they will have as your needs change.

SECTION 2: WHAT MOVES TO THE NEW HOME?

Once you have selected a new place, the next step is deciding what goes there. Think only of you; what you want and enjoy; what will turn your new space into your home. Ask yourself: Do I love it, where will it go, and is it useful?

Get a floor plan with room sizes and make extra copies so you can play around. Draw in the items you want to take. The communities' floor plans are to scale; so, if they show the bedroom with a double bed, two night stands and a dresser; that is what fits there.

You pay for square footage. Don't keep a bedroom for the kids. Get an inflatable air mattress or suggest they stay at a hotel where they can enjoy the pool.

SECTION 3: THE KIDS

Tell the kids that you are clearing out the house. Have a reasonable expectation of their time to help you.

Ask if they want anything. Tell them to speak now or forever hold their peace.

Agree together: Any gift belongs to the person receiving it. They can keep it, gift it, donate it or pass it along.

SECTION 4: CHORES TO DO
Keep track of the things you need to set-up and put phone numbers on the inside cover: Transfer newspaper; get address changed; call Realtor; call cable…

SECTION 5: THE AFTERMATH
What do you do with all the items left behind that neither you nor the children want?

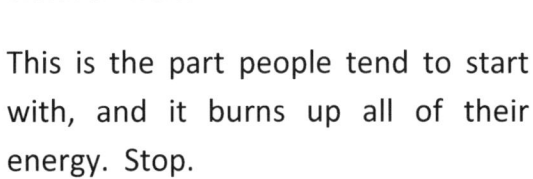

This is the part people tend to start with, and it burns up all of their energy. Stop.

How to liquidate what is left in your house depends on how much there is; also, the location; the cost to clean out and the value of what you are selling. A good senior move manager can help you decide what direction to take next.

Finally, take time to enjoy the great memories that will pop up as you are revisiting items you haven't seen for years.

23   Caregiving impacts you at work

Is taking care of your aging parents interfering with your job? You're not alone!

AARP reports that 40 percent of adults are caring for a family member who is sick or disabled. Most of those who are, don't even consider themselves to be a caregiver, thinking "I am a daughter/son/wife/parent, not a caregiver."

I realized that describes me. I am a caregiver. Are you?

In a recent seminar by the Fox Cities Chamber, entitled Aging Parents and the Workplace, the lead moderator was Steve Baue, owner ERC Counselors and Consultants. Baue had various statistics discussing what we are going through. He said that often the biggest problem for an employed caregiver isn't just taking care of their loved one, but also the added stress of how to keep-up with their job while they are doing it. They don't want to burden their co-workers.

Quoted was that the hours that caregiving demands take a toll on work:

- 39% have difficulty getting their work done on time

- 34% have had difficulty focusing at work

- 27% have had to miss work entirely

As an employer, you can decide that this is an unacceptable problem. Families and Work Institute and the Society for Human Resource Management report "some commonly held assumptions about flexibility in the workplace: Flexibility will be taken advantage of by workers; small employers can't afford flexibility; offering flexibility to low wage workers is not efficient and that there are no benefits of flexibility in high turnover industries."

The reality, FWI and SHRM report, is that "Not only does research disprove the above; it supports a link between retention and morale with flexibility."

One of our local businesses, Kimberly Clark, recognizes the impact that caregiving has on their employees. Rather than harp on productivity, they want to help their staff deal with these life-challenges. They have created an internal group called the Family Caregivers Network.

A participant of the Chamber seminar was Joel Hopper, ITS Business Analyst at KC. Hopper has a passion for helping his workplace members, as well as all of us, to find the best resources to deal with this challenge.

He shared with us tips on how an employer can help: Be an ally. Offer flexibility. Share information that can help. Work together with your employee to establish a plan.

Hopper also said that rather than being a problem, employees who are caregivers are the ones you want – they are the ones who "get it done".

Along the lines of sharing information, he had the resources that he considers to be so important that KC shares it with all of the folks in the Family Caregivers Network, and they would like to share it with you:

    www.aarp.org/home-family/caregiving/

    www.caregiveraction.org

    www.dhs.wisconsin.gov/adrc/

    www.liveandworkwell.com/

Two things that I heard for Family Caregivers: First, get support. Do you think no one gets what you are going through? There are people who do. Find them; they will make all the difference for you. Second, give yourself credit. You are doing the best you can at one of the toughest jobs there is.

24   Let's make Box-It Day a thing on December 26

To my grandchildren,

You told me how excited you are that Christmas is coming and you can't wait to see what Santa will bring. Me too! It is fun getting new things.

You've heard me say that some grownups have too many things in their house, that they just can't get rid of stuff.

Well, the two things actually go together. Over the years, people get new goodies, like for Christmas, for birthdays and lots of other times. When they bring new things into their house, they don't take the old items out. It goes on year after year, until one day, they have so much stuff that they don't know what to do with it all.

Keeping stuff is a habit - one that they started when they were little kids, like you are now.

Think about it. You already have so many toys, that it is a big job when Mom tells you to clean your room. After Christmas, you will have even more things to pick up, unless….

We could start a new tradition, you and me. For every new gift we get for Christmas, let's put something in a box. We'll fill the box and give it to people who aren't as blessed as we are.

Do you know that in Canada, in Australia, England, and even in Ireland, where your great-way-back grandparents came from, there is a holiday called Boxing Day? It is December 26, the day after Christmas. It's called Boxing Day because the kings and lords used to box up their Christmas leftovers and give them to their serfs and to the poor.

We'll borrow from their idea a bit. We also will do it on December 26. But let's call it Box-It Day.

We can even start ahead and begin gathering some stuff now. Ask Dad for a box. Clear some space in your toy chest for the new goodies that Santa will be bringing. Don't forget to look around for all the parts of the toys that you are gifting. Puzzles are better with all the pieces.

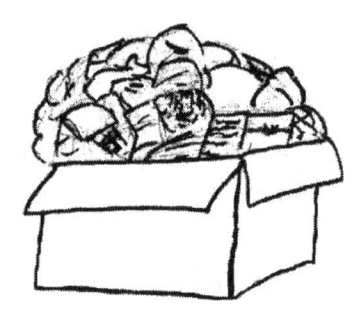

Before you know it, Christmas will be here. When you see all of your new toys under the tree, remember, before you take them to your room, let's put some old toys into that box, so we can give them to other kids. Yes, you can get rid of other stuff too, like old shoes and books, anything.

On Box-It Day, let's go together and deliver them to Goodwill or St. Vincent de Paul or wherever. You pick. It is a good feeling.

It isn't easy to let go of things that you've enjoyed. But now that you are getting big-kid things, maybe you can let go of some of your little-kid things.

We are so lucky. We have so much. Let's share.

Love, Grandma

P.S: Parents and grandparents, since we all are kids at heart, you can join in the new Box-It Day tradition too. Let's all do it together.

Out with the old and in with the new. Not just "In with the new."

25   Organize photos now to help 'generation gap' later

Dear Readers:

Here is a note I received from a friend, Chris Church. She has some good words for us:

"Who is this?"

"Not a clue!"

That was the conversation my sister and I had while going through hundreds of old photos from our parents who had died several years earlier.

Eventually, Chris Church identified these children as her grandfather and his two sisters.

While it's hard to decide who gets Mom's good silver or Dad's collection of antique clocks, that's nothing compared to going through and sorting a lifetime of photos—most of which aren't identified.

Last winter, I spent weeks going through boxes of photos from my parents. It was pretty easy identifying my grandparents, aunts, uncles and cousins. But there were dozens of people none of us could identify. I threw them away.

I came across one formal portrait of a young boy with two older girls, probably from the late 1800s. Thanks to the magic of email, I sent it out to my cousins to see if they knew who these people were.

Cousin Nick said it was my grandfather and his sisters. I would never have known.

So, while you urge your parents to sort through their other stuff, make it a priority to sit down, go through their photos with them and write some ID's on the back. It'll take a while, but it's worth it.

And here's the real kicker: Go through your own photos.

If you really want to leave a legacy to the people who come after you, your photos are a treasure trove. When your grandkids go through these in years to come, they'll love to see you when you wore bell-bottoms or had tie-dye shirts and hair down to your shoulders.

They won't care that much about your friends or neighbors, and I can guarantee they won't get weak in the knees with your scenic photos of the Grand Canyon or Yosemite. Clean out the excess.

By you investing time now, your kids, their kids, and the kids that come after them will have a photographic heritage of their past.

And that's priceless.

Reply from Jean:

Thanks, Chris.

Readers, some of you will express the opposite problem. You have the pictures, but none of the next generation wants them. Don't be so quick to throw out scrap books. You probably weren't as interested in history at 25 as you are at 60. Losing loved ones over the years brings nostalgia. It will for the next generation too.

Ways to deal with the stacks:

First, glean.

Take pictures using your smartphone. I did it at 90-year-old, Aunt Val's house last month. It works!

Host a cousins party, share stories and albums. Have a scanner there.

Have your pictures, videos, slides professionally copied and updated.

Here's another twist: Since we now store so many pictures on our computers, unless we do something about it now, when we are gone, so are our pictures. That will create a whole new kind of "generation gap".

26   Someone to watch over me

From Jean: The beginning of this one was written with a great deal of help from my sister, Julie Dobberstein. She was Dad's caregiver as he progressed through his final year with Alzheimer's. This one is dedicated to you, Julie.

Come and sit quietly with me. Have a cup of coffee. Hold my hand.

Some days I won't know you, yet some days I might.

Your time is most precious to me. Little do you know your strength calms me; tell me it will be alright.

Be patient with me. What is real to me may not be real to you. Others correct me and cause me such stress. You don't try to fix me, you just step into my world.

Keep your sense of humor. Your smile is calming. Your laugh warms my heart.

Have a "so what" attitude. When I keep folding papers, it's no big deal. I was a clerk in the army and I have to keep order. It isn't hurting anyone - just bring more papers.

Don't ask me multiple choice questions. Kindly decide things for me. You are my voice.

I worry about things that you cannot see. I think I am still at work and my chores aren't done. I fret and I fuss. Assure me that all is okay, that I've finished working for today and now it is time to relax.

Let's look at pictures; a colorful book. It may bring on memories or, today, maybe not. But sharing time with you brings me peace for a while.

Don't be loud or talk too fast. I've come to struggle to understand all that.

If I ask about someone who has passed away, don't tell me they are gone - they're just gone for today. Share a memory of them. Their closeness is what I long for.

It is good to be here where I am safe and well cared for.

I want to go "home" but what am I really searching for? It is peace. My mind is befuddled, that's what I want to escape. Don't try to reason with me or argue, just change the subject and soon we will move on.

Let me do the things I still can and help me along when I can't.

Let's listen to old songs or watch a show. Doesn't matter. Just don't go.

Sometimes I don't know you. You wonder if you should visit me. Yes. I still need a friend. Your voice belongs to someone I love. Your face is familiar, smile for me.

We can still share good times, take me for a walk.

If you can't be with me, don't feel guilty. Instead, make sure my world is being held together.

If I get upset, know it's not you. I don't do it on purpose.

I know you love me. I love you more.

This disease makes life a muddle, but who would have guessed that it could draw us closer together? I depend on you. I may not remember, but the gift you are giving me is something you'll never forget.

I've always been proud of my children, but seeing all that you're doing in my life, my heart would be near bursting with pride.

I am so grateful for all you do.

Love you,

Dad

27   Even in volunteer work, change can be difficult

Dear Jean:

We are a non-profit organization which relies greatly on our senior volunteer corps. It is a dedicated population, the likes of which we will probably never see again. Yet, there are times when we have volunteers who are no longer a good fit for the job that they consider "theirs". One long-standing volunteer is getting to be a bit cantankerous. We've talked to them about their declining hearing and tried putting them in back-room roles. They are unbending. They don't like technology and want to keep doing things the old way. This person is in a public area, meeting with visitors daily. Sometimes they make comments to visitors that are embarrassing.

Answer: There can be so many causes for a decline in abilities, from changes in health to frustration with things that have nothing to do with their job. The inability to understand technology makes many folks feel ignorant. As you had discussed, first you want to look for causes. When you have addressed that, it is time for a delicate but necessary conversation. Your job is the survival of your business.

I reached out to my "go to" guy for human resource questions, Jay Stephany. Stephany is the District Director of the WISHRM (Wisconsin Society of Human Resource Managers).

"Challenges in a volunteer setting are just like in the workplace. When you have people who are tenured and very passionate about their work, it is time to ask them 'What about your legacy?' What do you want to leave this organization when you retire or move on?"

Stephany said, "They had a chance to build that volunteer role to what it is today, and it is also important to talk about succession planning. More people need to know how to do that specific job. That person knows how to do it, but if they weren't there, suddenly all of that knowledge they brought to the organization would be gone."

"Celebrate all they have done in their role, but also ask them to Give the Gift." Stephany described Giving the Gift of Your Knowledge, as a way to pass on their legacy to someone else, to keep the organization strong by continuing what they created.

I mentioned to Stephany that the volunteer's response might be "But it's *my* job!". He said a good response might be, "Yes, it was your job and you've done wonderful with it. What are some of the other areas where we can now use your help?" Then transition them into non-customer facing roles.

"Sometimes you have to stick to your guns because you know it is the best move for the entire organization. Remember, your job is to be sure your customers have the best experience possible.

Don't avoid the difficult conversation. There are ways to tactfully talk about it. Ask them to help create the next leader. When all else fails, it is time to plan a great retirement party for them and celebrate all that they have done over the years."

28   Shredding old papers is part of protecting yourself

Many of you have a handy little shredder in your home. Great!

Those pint-sized shredders are perfect for the weekly shredding. Some of the things you may want to shred on a regular basis are credit card offers and all those outdated medical sheets that you get with every doctor visit.   You may want to shred receipts and deposit slips after you've checked them against your credit card or bank statement - unless you need them for taxes or warranties.

With all the threats to identity theft, you want to shred anything with your name, address, birth date, signature or identifiable account or social-security information on it.

Home shredders are ideal for staying ahead of that mountain of stuff that comes through your door.

Want to simplify? For bills, consider electronic payments (ACH), or you can do "bill pay" through your bank/credit union. They will even help you set it up.

It's great for regular bills like insurance, water, electric, mortgage, cable, phone, newspaper and your church.

I have a "billing" account at my financial institution. With just one deposit each month, all those regular bills are taken care of. Not only does it save me work, but it is more secure because my account information doesn't go out on checks.

The bonus is that it is done automatically. My payments are never late. No stamps are needed.

If your child helps you pay your bills and has asked you to do this, hear them out. If you are holding out because the only time you see them is when they pay your bills, that isn't a good reason. It is controlling. Wouldn't you rather they spend those two hours with you doing something else?

Now, those are great ideas for that little shredder, but let's talk about that gigantic pile of old papers that you have in your house.

When you are cleaning out a quarter-century of paperwork, quit trying to run it through that poor little shredder. What a waste of your time. If you've tried it, you know the shredder isn't very happy either. It keeps turning off because it gets tired.

Have you had a box full of papers to shred, sat for an hour shredding, only to find that the box is still ¾ full and you are numb? Then you realize you still have 3 more boxes. I get tired just thinking about it.

We are talking about a super-size shredding job. Stop.

Call your financial institutions and ask if they have a free shredding day. Many do.

If you don't want to haul it there, call a shredding company. Ask what they charge to come to your house and shred a load. You may be pleasantly surprised. For about $50 - $100, you can get roughly 10 boxes done. It gives you peace of mind because you see them shred it – in just about 12 minutes.

Want to split the cost? Ask your friend or neighbor if they have things to shred too.

For this really big job, you are worth the investment.

29 Seeing primary doctor is important as you age

Dear Jean,

My mother-in-law is 76 years old. She lives by herself in a small town in northern Wisconsin, about 100 miles from us. She gets her medical care in our city. Over the last year she has struggled with some chronic problems including migraines, shoulder pain and pain in her side.

I asked if she would like me to accompany her to her appointments. She doesn't advocate well for herself, and I could see things were not moving in a positive direction.

After we went to her first appointment together, at a pain clinic, I began to question her about her symptoms, tests and doctors she had seen. My husband and I have now learned that she has seen multiple orthopedic surgeons, gastroenterologists, rheumatologists, neurologists and more. She has had MRIs, x-rays, scans, etc.

She sees one doctor until they tell her something she doesn't like. One doctor does not communicate with another. She hasn't had a physical in over a year and has no on-going relationship with one physician.

I am so frustrated at her inability to stick with one thing or make any decisions. Ma is not disabled and cognitively she is fine. My husband thinks she may be depressed. She lives a very isolated life.

My husband instructed her to ask one of her daughters who they see for internists, and if they like their doctor, she should make an appointment with that doctor for a full physical. Nothing was done.

We don't know what to do. Getting the whole family together to make decisions is not a possibility as everyone has their own opinion.

Do you have any suggestions??

Answer: How frustrating for all of you, including your MIL, who is obviously looking for answers too.

I chatted with my own doctor about these challenges. Dr. Kelli Heindel said that your situation emphasizes the little appreciated benefit of a primary care physician - one person to know her history and to sift through conflicting opinions (including those of her own family members).

Does she have a "go-to" person, whether in the family or a friend? Can they encourage her to go to a primary care doctor? She may be more receptive knowing she would actually save time and money by not duplicating tests that aren't getting her closer to relief from pain.

Many seniors are stubbornly independent and proud of it. Perhaps you can take a different approach.

A great source for help is the Aging and Disability Resource Center (ADRC), in the county she lives in. They can help with this problem and many other challenges too, including isolation.

Their goals are to:

- Educate and empower people to remain independent as long as possible
- Help people understand their choices and make informed decisions
- Help people conserve their personal finances
- Reduce the demand for long-term care public funding

They say: "We have a team of specialists who are waiting to help *you* – free of charge, regardless of your income. We'll give you information, help you understand what resources are available, and help you decide what is best for you."

30   Falls are preventable with a little bit of education

Dear Jean: Twice this month, my mom has taken a fall; once stepping out of the bath and once outside on the ice. She had taken a class through Thompson Community Center on falling and because of that she knew how to get herself up. It was a 10-minute process on the ice, but she did it.

This would be a really good class to recommend to other people her age. I'm glad she didn't break anything. Just a few bruises.

Response: It's great to hear your mom was OK. Did you know that 1 in 3 people over 65 will fall this year? They are the leading cause of serious injuries. Falls don't just happen to frail, older people and they aren't a normal part of aging. Falls are preventable. There are many things you can do to reduce the possibility that you will fall.

The class you are referring to is called Stepping On and it is free. I assumed that it was a class about being careful. Wow, was I wrong. It is so much more, and it is available well-beyond our own community.

The National Council on Aging talks about this class, saying: "Stepping On is a multifaceted falls-prevention program for the community-residing elderly. About 30% of older people who fall lose their self-confidence and start to go out less often. Inactivity leads to social isolation and loss of muscle strength and balance, increasing the risk of falling. Stepping On aims to break that cycle, engaging people in a range of relevant fall preventive strategies."

Nancy Krueger, health and wellness coordinator directs the classes through the Aging and Disability Resource Center. She explained that at the Stepping On workshop, you will get professional advice from a physical therapist, a pharmacist, vision expert and a community-safety police officer.

Their goal is to reduce falls and build confidence in older people. These workshops provide a safe and fun experience focused on improving balance and strength, vision, home and environmental safety and a medication review.

"Stepping On" has been proven to reduce your risk of falls by up to 50 percent, according to Krueger. In just seven sessions, you can be stronger and steadier wherever you go.

"What basic things can we do today to be safe?" I asked Krueger. She answered that the biggest offender, by far, is hurrying. Don't rush to answer that phone. Take your time. Hurrying is almost always the primary cause of falling. The second offender is poor lighting; third is that if you don't have to go out in the bad weather, don't; and finally, always have one hand secure when changing surfaces. That means when you go down the steps, always use the handrail. As you are getting out of the tub or shower, hold that grab bar. It isn't for you to grab as you fall, it is for you to grab so you won't fall.

Krueger encourages: Falls ARE preventable – Don't wait until a fall injures more than your pride!

31 Don't be afraid to dig into your closet

Today, let's look at all the clothes in your closet. For some of you, it is plural - closets.

When my customers take me through their homes, as they start to downsize, they open their master bedroom closet and let out a big sigh. Ugh. So many clothes. Years of clothes. Decades even.

They don't know where to start. Just thinking about trying on all of those clothes to see what fits; it is exhausting.

Folks explain by saying something like "I used to be a (fill in the blank), so I needed these clothes for work."

Today's question is: How many hangers do you need? And, yes, by "hangers" we really mean clothes on hangers.

Here is how to attack that closet. You will only need a batch of black garbage bags and determination.

First, remove all the empty hangers and put them in a garbage bag. By getting rid of those extra hangers you are saying, "Never again will something come into this closet unless something else goes out."

Second, count the remaining hangers and answer: I have _____ hangers of clothes.

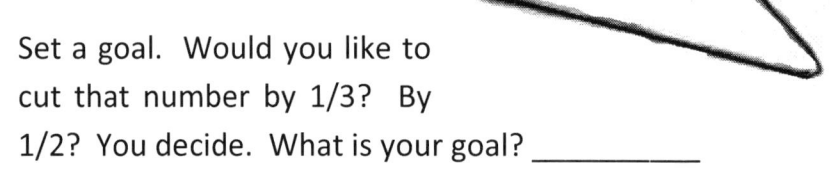

Set a goal. Would you like to cut that number by 1/3? By 1/2? You decide. What is your goal? _____

Next, slide a garbage bag over a hanger and make a hole for the hook of the hanger, then hang it in the closet as your divider. On the left side of the hanger, put all the clothes that you have actually worn in the past year; the things you have worn around the house or to an occasion. It doesn't matter if they are beat-up, faded or boring. If you have worn them, they go on the left.

These are you real clothes. This is, in fact, your wardrobe.

All the rest are extras. They are not actually part of your wardrobe. You don't wear them, right?

It is time to deal with those extras. If you've had them for over a year and they still have price tags on them, out they go.

Is the zipper broken? Buttons missing? Again, if you haven't fixed them in a year, into the bag.

Next, if you have clothes from a job you have retired from, it is time to retire those clothes.

If you don't like some of the clothes on the left, and have nicer ones on the right side, you can trade with yourself, but bag the ones you take from the left.

Next are the clothes that are two sizes too big or too small. Lighten your load, let them go.

No cheating. No keeping those tiered hangers that hold five skirts, nor putting three pair of pants on one hanger.

No fair eliminating hangers by getting rid of your spouse's items. However, you may encourage your spouse to join you on this quest.

How many hangers do you have now? _____

Those bags of clothes won't go to waste. Take them to a consignment store or to your favorite charity. Local families are waiting for your generosity.

Dear Reader: Take a moment, right now, to look up when daylight savings starts. Mark your calendar so that when you turn your clocks back an hour for daylight savings time, you will also change your smoke alarm batteries and update your File of Life information. Kids, offer to do this for your parents. No one over 70 should be on a ladder. To request a free File of Life kit, call the ADRC at 866-739-2372.

32   Lots to be thankful for, even as we age

"Thanksgiving is just around the corner. What can we be thankful for as we age?"

That was the question I posed to a pal of mine, Kathy Keene, host of the Good Neighbor Show on WHBY radio.

With 34 years on-air, Kathy has a faithful following of listeners. She is such a kind and sharing person. You can hear her smiles. Her deep laugh is contagious. She cares.

What you don't see on the radio is a vibrant woman who is approaching her 70th birthday.

Relaxing in her kitchen, on a beautiful autumn afternoon, I asked: What can we be thankful for as we age? Smiling, she told me that rather than complaining about the inevitable effects of aging, like more body aches and pains, diminishing eyesight and weight gain, she instead takes a line from the song "Don't worry, be happy".

Perhaps in her answers, you will remember some things that you are grateful for.

Things that I'm grateful and thankful for as I age

by Kathy Keene

"I am thankful for good health. Health is something you never think about until it's compromised. Even if your health isn't great, it could be worse and you likely still have some working parts to be thankful for.

I am thankful for the colors of each season. Being able to step outside to breathe in fresh air is a good reminder of how many little things we should be thankful for. Keeping your mind active is important for good health. Reading, doing crossword puzzles, visiting with family and friends and quilting. I'm thankful I am still able to do these things as I age.

Laughter! I am thankful for people who make me laugh. Without laughter, the world would be a sad place. Be thankful for the laughter of children, a spouse or friends.

I am thankful for not feeling guilty when I say "no". Sometimes we can't do all that is asked of us, and it is OK to say no.

I am thankful for my sweet little cat Belle. Pets offer one of the best examples of unconditional love.

Having a home. Whether you live in an apartment, a condo, retirement facility or own a house, having a place to call home is something to be thankful for.

Remembering your grandmother when you get out the heirloom china. Be grateful that you have a wonderful memory of a loved one.

Friends. We meet many people throughout our lives; some we keep, some we let go and some will simply become like family.

We can be thankful in every period of life, but we must realize that thankfulness changes as we grow older.

The older we get and the more we simplify our lives, even the most mundane things are a reminder to be thankful. Focus on the few things that matter in life, make each day count, and aim for a life that grows more beautiful, not more busy, through the years."

Now you can see why we call Kathy Keene the Good Neighbor!

33   Clearing out parents' home comes with big emotions

If one were writing a book on how to clear out an estate, it could also be entitled "How to break up a family."

Whether it is the family house that you were raised in, or their assisted-living apartment, emptying out your parents' home is one of the most emotional times that a family will go through. The result can either leave pleasant memories or bitter feelings that some family members never get over.

How to break-up a family:

One person decides for everybody. They know how to do it "best" and so they do it their way.

Surely, you are aware that your siblings have different personalities.

Peter Practical. "We can't afford to pay rent for even one extra day, so we have to get this stuff out." He may rent a truck and get it all moved out in one day, probably benefiting Goodwill or his kids. But the job is done.

Suzy Sentimental. She can't part with anything because it all has so much meaning. She wants every item to find the right home. She can't move forward.

Swoopin' Sarah. Just comes in and takes what she wants. She figures it is just stuff and isn't worth anything anyway.

Too Busy Tyler. He is an important man and can't get away from work. He is busy until September – or January. Meanwhile, every week the house sits, it costs money, work and worry for someone.

Debbie Denial. She is having a hard time accepting this. She has a myriad of excuses about why it can't be done now.

Yes, it is just "stuff", but it is also stuff that is infused with a lifetime of warm memories.

Many families have shared their "clean out" experiences with me, good and bad. The overriding theme of what worked best was that they worked together. As a family, they set goals. As a family, they decided what was fair. As a family, they got it done.

Peter Practical: You can be practical in more than one way. You were probably chosen as the financial person because you watch the money. Ask your siblings to set a reasonable timeframe to get the process completed, even if it means paying rent at Mom's apartment a little longer. Isn't family harmony worth the cost?

Suzy Sentimental : I get it. Mom and Dad's items are special but put emphasis on the items that have special meaning to you. Work on the cherished few, rather than the overwhelming many.

Swoopin' Sarah: Whoa! Those items have significance to the others too. Wait your turn.

Too Busy Tyler – Yes, we are all busy. But are you saying that you are too busy to help your brothers and sisters with something that is a great burden to them, even if it isn't to you? Make time.

It is about balance. Be respectful of all people involved – from the sentimental to the practical. It is also about getting it done in a timely fashion and allowing everyone to move forward. You can do this – together.

34   Educate aging parents about charity scams

Dear Jean: Last week, when visiting my Mom, I found a stack of "charity" requests. These sad appeals ranged from wounded vets to starving orphans. They looked bogus to me. Mom wouldn't even discuss the possibility that they might be a con. The letters and pictures were very convincing. She is positive that they are legit. She has all kinds of freebies from them; mailing labels, calendars and stationery.

I think we should monitor her mail and get her off the lists. When I tried to get my siblings to help, I was met with a lot of resistance.

It is plain and simple theft! It makes me angry. What can I do?

Answer: "Seniors are ripe pickings for con artists," I was told, by Teri Rose, a certified identity theft risk management specialist.

Rose was pretty blunt when I asked her about your problem. She answered: "The hard truth is scammers look for easy prey. While no one is immune, the characteristics of easy victims include being naive and unsuspecting, a sense of duty, poor organizational habits, ego and greed (something for free)."

"We all like to feel important. It makes us feel good to contribute to a worthy cause, but the hard truth is we may only be their victim."

"Scammer tactics include exploiting authority roles, using official looking certificates to make you feel important, including pictures that appeal to your heart and using copy-cat names that sound like a legitimate cause. While it looks personal and official, it's easy and quick to print. You are only a sucker on their list."

Using a mix of ideas from Rose, and from Charity Navigator, here are some strategies to share with your mom:

- She is a victim. Don't attack her choices. That only causes her to be defensive and makes her a victim again.
- Do your homework. Check out charities at www.CharityNavigator.org. It is free.
- Educate her. Encourage her to talk with friends and family. Discuss the latest scams, and review appeal letters. Share how to tell it is a scam.

- Talk about planning her donations. Fake appeals are all about getting pushovers to shell out money. Discuss what her core values are and help her decide which charities match her desires.
- Then help her get removed from marketing mail lists.
- Say no! Intrusions into your home, your phone, your mail, your computer steal your time and money. You owe them nothing.
- Don't get flustered. Practice phone call scenarios that she might receive and how she might handle them. Scammers use pressure tactics. If you have a plan, it will be easier to cut them off quickly.
- Don't let them pick your pocket. If you are about to give your credit card number or Social Security number to <u>anyone</u> who called you, hang up.

Not only do scammers steal your money, but they keep you from helping the very people you actually wanted to help.

Finally, to quote the Better Business Bureau: "Oh, and if it sounds too good to be true, it most likely is."

35   Sort as you decorate for the seasons

Today's topic: How to smile with satisfaction knowing that you planned ahead.

Someday, you may decide to move to smaller, more manageable quarters, perhaps a senior community. When you move, you'll look at your mountain of holiday decorations and think "I wish I would have known about this move last year; I would have put away my decorations better. It would have saved me a lot of time."

When someone is downsizing, they can be overwhelmed by the workload that it takes to sort through all their possessions and decide which items to take to their new home.

One of the tasks will be to select your favorite do-dads to decorate your new apartment. Why not tackle that job now, while you are decorating your house for the seasons? It is October. There are several holidays right around the corner.

Most senior apartments have a storage locker. It is the perfect place to put some personal knick-knacks that you change out from time to time.

Get four storage totes. The clear ones are nice because you can see the contents. Totes are preferable over boxes because they keep things dry.

Let's use one for autumn, two for the holidays, and one for spring.

You aren't actually going to fill them now. There will be three steps.

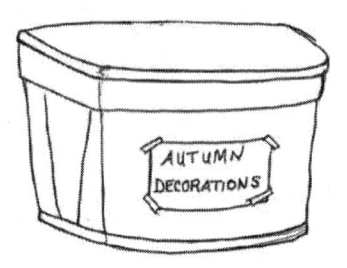

First, once you have decorated for the season; look at what is leftover in your collection. If it wasn't good enough to decorate with this year, consider eliminating it altogether. The charities await your generosity.

Second is enjoying. October is time for the fall harvest, Halloween, Thanksgiving, and Sukkot. Go ahead and decorate your house for the season, enjoy.

Third, once the fall season is over, while you still have everything out, you mindfully put it away, packing into the "future" tote, the special items that you would want to keep if you downsize. Picture an imaginary apartment and what you might decorate it with. Think small-scale. Label your tote Autumn.

When winter rolls around, do the same, but perhaps one tote isn't enough. Surely there will be room in that imaginary storage locker for two totes for the Christmas holidays. Do you celebrate Hanukkah? Then make a tote for your Menorah and other holiday accoutrements.

Honestly, you won't have room in your next home for all the decorations you currently put out in your house, but then you won't have an entire house to decorate. Save items that are smaller scale: tabletop decorations, knick-knacks for shelves; maybe an 18" wreath for your future door, rather than a 48" wreath for the front of your current house.

Now, you'll have a tote for autumn harvest, two totes for winter. Make a fourth tote, for spring (St. Patrick's, St. Valentine's Day, Easter, Passover, pinks, pastels, chicks, and tulips).

With good planning, you can make your next home just as charming and decked out as your current house.

Even as we move into smaller spaces, it is still fun to express ourselves with items that reflect our style and bring us pleasure.

36   Program welcomes those with dementia

My business has a Purple Angel. Does yours?

Perhaps you are wondering, what is a Purple Angel? It is a designation given to establishments that are committed to providing "hospitality and support to customers contending with memory loss, confusion or other symptoms associated with dementia."

The short version of that is "dementia friendly".

Having a Purple Angel on your door tells caregivers and folks with dementia that they will receive compassion and respect, and extra help if they need it. It says "Welcome!"

The Purple Angel program trains your employees to understand the needs of people with memory loss. Just making small changes in the way you address someone can make a big difference to them; making your interaction more relaxing and enjoyable for both of you. Win-Win.

What did it take for training? John McFadden, memory-care ambassador extraordinaire, came to our office and met with the crew (movers and office staff). He talked about the special needs of those with memory loss.

The biggest message I have learned is that choices are frustrating and sometimes downright stressful.

In customer service, we have always been trained to give customers many choices and let them decide what most fits their wants and desires.

With dementia, peace and comfort is the desire. Choices cause frustration, so let's stop requiring unnecessary choices.

Help them make their choices. And, no, I didn't say take away their choices. There is a difference.

Some examples: If you are a waitress, don't offer a litany of specials. Offer a good option – "Our meatloaf is delicious today. Would you like that?" If it isn't something they want, they'll let you know.

For my employees, who are professional movers, it shouldn't be: "Where would you like the sofa?" My guys have a good eye and may know that the TV will go by the cable outlet, so the sofa will probably go on the long wall opposite. They might say: "I think the sofa will look good here. Is that OK with you?"

People with dementia and memory loss still want control of their world. They know what pleases them but making choices from multiple options is frustrating. Keep it simple.

What is the benefit to your company? Our population is aging; these are our customers, this is us. Isn't it your desire as a business to give your customers the most comfortable experience possible? It sure is mine.

Dementia is a progressive disease. People with early stages of dementia are engaged in our community, as they should be. Like others with a disability, they want to be respected for their abilities and remain as independent as possible for as long as possible. We are part of the Purple Angel program because it helps folks remain active and contributing to our community.

Isn't that what community is all about?

Are you willing to commit?

WE ARE DEMENTIA AWARE

37   The New Year is a time for change... or is it?

When you are with Mom and Dad, put aside your fast-paced ways and slow down a little.

Your parents' home is their comfort zone. They are content there because nothing changes. As eyesight and energy fades, they are still cozy because they know where everything is. It is their nest. Then you stopover.

Do you breeze into your parents' world and want to change things? Have you decided that it is time for a new chair, or you want to clean out their pantry or rearrange the living room because it is boring? That is so disruptive to their peace.

A different way you could visit your parents is to take a deep breath and settle in. Go and enjoy the time you are spending with them, and let them enjoy it, too. Instead of putting them in a dither, just s-l-o-w d-o-w-n. We do this thing called "multi-tasking" and seem quite proud of our ability to do so.

To our parents, it is exhausting. They are conditioned to start and finish a task before moving on to the next thing. Not only is it part of their make-up, but as folks age, it may take a little longer to complete something. Trying to rush them, or doing several things at once, can be frustrating for them, and for us, too, because they don't keep up.

If you are helping them pay bills, just sit down together and finish that task before moving on to the next project.

If there is a change that you think will help them, tell them your suggestion, explain why it will help, show them two or three times; walk through it. Discuss it together and ask their permission to try it. Don't just steamroll them with your choices.

If Mom is not taking her meds correctly, how can you help solve it, together? If you come up with a solution and she isn't on board, it isn't going to happen once you leave.

If Dad isn't getting the bills paid on time, can you work with him to get more organized, perhaps setting up some ACHs or auto pay, or you write the checks and he signs them?

Also, when you are at their home, put things back! If you get out the cards to play a game, put them back where you found them. Of course, Mom has been telling you this all of your life, but now it takes on new significance. She has her habits and her patterns; they make her life relaxing. Upsetting her order disturbs her world.

What isn't relaxing is that phone call you get an hour after you leave. She is in a frenzy because her checkbook is missing. You left it on the kitchen table. If that isn't where you found it, you shouldn't have left it there.

When you go visit, you can be a disruption, or you can make life easier by helping them.

38   Great gift ideas for your aging parents, grandparents

Dear Jean,

I recently bought your book, "Transitions – stories of how to help Mom and Dad with their stuff". Almost daily I have a constant anxiety about my stuff. I just finished the chapter "Shopping for Elderly Parents? We've got Answers" and wish you'd run it in the paper again – with a headline that will grab adult children's/grandkid's attention. I get lovely gifts from my family – but – those gifts are among the stuff that I'll have to be sorting through, possibly getting rid of. – Signed, Too Much Already

Dear Too Much,

Here you go, along with some updates.   The original question was: "What do we get Grandma and Grandpa for Christmas? They say they don't want or need anything, yet we still want to show we care."

I asked readers. Here are their responses. No one mentioned fancy coffee makers, electronics or general "stuff".

A common suggestion was gift cards: Cards for groceries, hair salon/barber and for the pharmacy to help with copays.

One gent responded: "We still give my 95-year-young mother-in-law gift certificates to her favorite eating places. She loves to eat out, and even though we treat most of the time, she still likes to pull out a gift certificate and say, 'Let me buy dinner tonight.'"

For the techie senior: A gift card for Nook books or iTunes gift cards for music downloads.

Another favorite is single-serving food, also soups, brownies and cookies. One gal said: "My parents always loved home-cooked meals, frozen and ready to microwave, especially as it got harder for Dad to see to cook and for Mom to stand long enough to cook."

If they live in a community, consider gift certificates for additional meals and "banked" money for outside trips.

One friend said: "When my grandma was in the nursing home, I would massage her hands with her favorite lotion. It kept her hands nice; it was a way to connect through touching and it was a scent she enjoyed."

More: Puzzles, stamps, box of birthday cards and thank you notes, easy crossword puzzle books, personalized calendars with birthdays and family events already noted.

Give your parents the gift of independence with the push-the-button-for-help units. It can make them feel safe and allow them to remain in their house.

Help around the house was a huge response. Offer your assistance to clean closets, cook a meal, spring-clean, shampoo carpets, clean windows, change furnace filters or balance their checkbook and pay bills.

Not surprisingly, the number one request was giving the gift of you.

Make a coupon book and say you will: Call them every Tuesday morning, take them to Friday fish, do weekly shopping trips, take them to their Sunday church service, have a movie night at their home complete with DVDs and popcorn, play cards/games, or bring grandchildren to visit.

Then do it.

Share this with your kids and encourage them to give Grandma and Grandpa something they can really use and enjoy. This Christmas, give a gift from the heart.

39   Consider bits of your history to pass on

Have your kids told you they don't want any of your "stuff"? Maybe that is because you are trying to give them things you collected, but that aren't special to them.   Hint: If it was a "collectible", it is probably not.

What are the gems they might actually care about? First, try asking them. Then think about tradition and history. Terri Benincasa, Host of Boomer Nation, gathered this great list of personal items. She suggests you make a small box of treasures to share with them. I suggest you also attach a note that tells them the story. Here are some of her ideas:

Your first passport
Looking at all those country stamps from your trip bumming around Europe staying at youth hostels will remind them of what an adventurer you are. It also opens the door to telling or retelling the stories.

Military discharge papers
Aside from the very practical aspect that your children may one day need them to help you get services from the Department of Veteran Affairs, looking at old papers with old dates on them is infinitely cool. One more important thing with this one: gets us talking about Vietnam, which must never be forgotten lest it be repeated.

A printed and framed wedding photo
Digital photography is fine, but there is just something importantly visceral about a printed photo. Don't worry if yours is showing its age; in the case of old photos, that's precisely the point. And, if you're divorced, that's OK...they still deserve a pic of Mom and Dad when it all began for them.

Something belonging to the oldest relative they knew
Make it small but personal. Giving them something from a relative they knew at some point, is cool. Also, something from a family member many generations ago might be well received, particularly when accompanied by a terrific tale about that person.

A sentimental piece of jewelry
It may be the ring you got at your Sweet 16 or the watch you received from your dad when you graduated college. Its value lies in its sentiment, not just dollar signs. My brother continues to wear Daddy's watch even though it's not an

expensive timepiece. Good jewelry might be great to hand down while you're still alive, so long as each child gets one and they're beyond the point of needing to sell it for rent money.

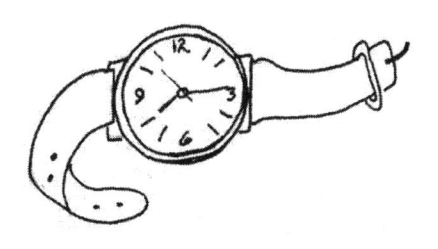

Photo of the first time you held them
While you probably have a zillion baby pictures, the first one is the keeper.

Things from their childhood
Not the ubiquitous Little League trophies, early artwork or those hand prints in paint. Think report cards, especially if there are teachers' comments on them, or their college letter of acceptance.

Tags worn by their childhood pet(s)
Our furry family members deserve to be remembered as well. Rusty's name tag has a place in the remembrances box, along with a photo of him with the family.

These are gifts to cherish.

40   Caring for aging senior? Here's where to find help

Ah, Christmas; a time for loved ones and eating and gifts and giving.

It is also a time for visiting with family we haven't seen for a while. While you are together for the holidays, keep your eyes open for signs that all is well in their world.

Seniors, maybe this is a good time to sit down with your adult children and have a heart-to-heart talk with them. Share your concerns about maintaining your house and ask them to help you keep control of your life.

Boomers, are you becoming increasingly worried about your parents staying in their house, but you have no idea where to turn? It is particularly difficult if you live far away.

There is a place to get help, and it is free.

The Aging and Disability Resource Center (ADRC): Doesn't that name sound exactly like what you want? A resource. In

Wisconsin, every county and every tribe has a connection to an ADRC.

Call them, talk to them, and meet with them. If you can't get in to their office, they can come to you for a home visit. Free. They will even do a conference call to include out-of-state family members.

They will speak with you, listen to your story, and can also give you options to consider. They don't make decisions for you; they guide you. The choices are yours. They are unbiased, and they aren't family.

In keeping with the Twelve Days of Christmas, let me share just twelve of the multitudes of tools you can find help with at the ADRC:

- ➤ Help cut the "red tape" with assistance filling out Medicare forms, Medicaid, Social Security, Senior Care Enrollment, housing and utility issues, forms, forms, forms.
- ➤ Options for home delivered meals and locations of community meal sites
- ➤ Connections for help with chores, companionship, health care, in-home personal care
- ➤ Help getting your affairs in order: Will, Health Care Power of Attorney, Living Will, Financial Power of Attorney
- ➤ Help preserving your family's nest egg, your financial resources

- Connections to support groups
- Useful suggestions about choosing an assisted living/nursing home facility
- Timely information – if you eventually must go on Family Care or Medicaid, there are things you need to have in order, otherwise you may not get your long-term care as soon as you need it.
- Respite help for the main caregiver
- Safety – is the home safe? What extra steps that you can take to ensure you can stay in the house longer?
- Solutions for transportation if driving has become a challenge
- Directory of services for seniors, and so much more.

They will make it easy for you.

The ADRC is there to help you *"Live Your Best Possible Life".* Whether you are facing the challenges of aging and/or disability or caring for someone who is, they've got what you are looking for. Free.

Make the Aging and Disability Resource Center your first step to take and first call to make. What a wonderful gift.

> There are ADRCs in every county of Wisconsin. Check the county directory where the senior lives.

41   Collections often have great value... but not financial

Dear Jean: My mom has many collectables, including Norman Rockwell plates, Franklin Mint gold coins, Hummel plates and much more. She says they are worth a lot. I wonder. How do we find out what the value is?

Answer: I sat down for an education with Greg Willett of Greg Willett Antiques & Estate Sale Services. "Is any of it collectable?" I asked.

"Don't confuse 'collectable' with 'valuable'," he answered. "Sure, it is collectable. People collect them. But the question should be, is it valuable/sellable?" When asked that, his answer was: "For those types of items, there is little to no market for 99 percent of it. You're lucky if you have that 1 percent that brings in something close to what you paid for it. Certainly, there are always exceptions, but they are few and far between."

"The plate collections, that everyone was so enamored with started at $70 or $100. They even promoted collector clubs.

Now, there are no or very few buyers. If you can get $10, you are fortunate."

As for the gold coins bought from magazine ads, he asked: "First of all, are they really gold, or do they use words like 'layered in gold' or 'clad in gold'? Those are just fancy names to say they have a gold wash on them. Certainly, sterling silver and karat gold are valuable (10, 14, 18k)."

One way to determine the value is to go to eBay. Put in the exact item by name, then advance search and click on sold listings. That will tell you what items actually sold for, rather than what people have them listed for. It is an idea of where the item is valued on a worldwide market. Then you have to factor in the work of selling and shipping it.

If your mom is disappointed by what you find, remind her of the pleasure her hobby gave her in collecting and displaying her treasures over the years. That is where the real value is.

Dear Jean: Our parents have to move in the next few months.

How do we kids (six of us) unite and help them work through all the items they have acquired over their lifetime?   Mom has put items on a table saying – take it, if you want it. We don't all live in the same city or state that she does. Some of us have an interest in the same items. Others have already asked and taken specific (special) items without the rest of us siblings knowing about it.

We have various personalities types, with some siblings saying "bring in the dumpster!" and others that are more sensitive to Mom and Dad's memories. Can you recommend some guidelines or ways it's worked for others (lottery system, putting names on items of interest, having an estate/auction and the kids bidding on items, etc.)? How do we deal with meddling in-laws or grandchildren's' spouses stepping in?

Readers: Do you have suggestions for this family? What worked or didn't work for you? Let me know and I'll share.

42   Benefits available to wartime vets

Readers,

We recently received a request to rerun this information. Veterans: This one is for you.

Today, I'd like to discuss a benefit for wartime vets that many are not aware of. It is the veterans pension.

For several years, I helped my buddy Phil with his finances. He lived on Social Security. They say you shouldn't plan to live off just Social Security, but the reality is that many do.

Phil would get his check on the 5th. We'd pay the rent and utilities, pay something on his never-ending medical bills, and buy prescriptions, bus passes and groceries.

On that budget, buying the little things is tough; like a small Christmas gift for his grandchildren, an evening out with friends or new shoes.

Phil often teased about how he wished we could stretch it further so he could buy more of his Achilles' heel, Pepsi.

Sadly, a month after Phil died, I learned of the Veterans Pension. If you are eligible for it, I don't want you to miss the opportunity Phil did.

Roughly, here are some factors for determining if you are eligible:

1) Veteran's Pension is for veterans, spouses and surviving spouses of service members who served at least 1 day during a war period. They did not have to serve in the country of the war.

2) Veteran is over 65 or disabled.

3) Must show financial need. Some of the main factors are: Low income, assets under $80,000 (they don't count your house) and medical expenses.

Yes, it starts out as simple as that.

Simple? Yes. Easy? No.

No one will come looking for you to give you this money. You must apply for it. Based on this brief information, don't decide if you qualify or not. Ask.

The paperwork can be tedious. But if you get $1,000-$2,000 a month, isn't it worth it? Even if the process takes a while, they pay retroactive to when you applied.

I spoke with Attorney Drew MacDonald, who you may know for his work with the Old Glory Honor Flight. He suggested that you get an experienced advocate because at 70 to 90 years old, you may not be equipped to handle the paperwork at this juncture of your life. MacDonald is certified through the

VA to help file for VA benefits. He said you should never pay a fee to an attorney, or anyone, to help you file.

Contact your County Veterans Service Office (CVSO). Their job is to help veterans and their families obtain veterans benefits, and they are happy to do so. It's not free money – you've earned it.

Looking back on the last years with Phil, and how he accepted the hardships that came his way, it would have been such a relief to have had more money; he may have even been able to keep the refrigerator stocked with Pepsi!

Make it a point to find out if you might be eligible and apply for the Veterans Pension. And to all of you veterans out there, THANK YOU.

Additional note from Jean: After this column was published, Joe Aulik from the Winnebago County Veterans Services Office contacted me. He asked to add some clarifications:

- The Veterans' Pension helps in offsetting your medical expenses.

- Liquid assets need to be under $80,000 (they don't count your house or car), this includes checking, savings, IRA accounts, CDs, stocks, bonds etc.

- Your monthly income (Social Security, Private Pensions, IRA distributions etc.) reduced with *monthly medical* expenses need to fall below certain VA thresholds.

- If you are eligible, and depending on your level of healthcare needs, the maximum a married veteran can obtain from the VA is $25,448 or $19,710 for a single veteran (As of 7/2016)

43   Senior centers have "everything A-Z"

Dear Jean: My mother has lost many friends over the years. She is the last of her brothers and sisters. She is so isolated at home and won't discuss moving. I've suggested that she check out the local senior center. She said all they do is play cards and that she isn't old enough for that place (she is 79). Does a senior center have programs to help keep her engaged?

Answer: Too funny! Mom used to say the same thing, and then one day she went to the Thompson Community Center for a computer class. Then she signed up for chair-yoga. Then choir. She was hooked. Now, nothing gets in the way of her "me time". She loves it there.

The local senior centers have everything from A to Z. Literally:

Alzheimer's Association, adult day services, AA, advocacy, AddLife centers

Bingo, billiards, Bible study, bus trips, blood pressure screening, bunko, bridge

Computer classes, consulting, Celebrating Caregivers, Civic League, cup of coffee, conversation

Diabetes screens, dancing, donations

Energy, euchre, emotional support, education, experience

Flu shots, fun, foot care, friends

Good times, grill outs, games, guidance

Health and Wellness Clinic, Hallelujah Chorus, Hearing-Loop

Imagination, ice cream, internet

Joking around, jazz, joy

Knitting, kindness, kids

Laughter, library, line dancing, lunch, leisure

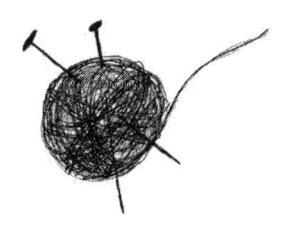

Memory Café, meditation, music, meals, memory loss resources

Newsletters, notes, neighbors

Options, older adult services

Paint the Masters, pinochle, programs that can help you, popcorn

Quilting, ac**Q**uaintances

~ 170 ~

Referrals, respite, rest and relaxation

Seniors, singing, Spanish, stimulation, Silver Sneakers Stretch, socializing

Take Five, Texas Hold'em

Upcoming events, understanding, United Way 211

Volunteers, veterans, visually impaired support group

Windows computer class, woodcarving, writing class, Wii, walking club

e**X**ercising, Xtra care

Yoga, YMCA, Young at Heart Singers

Zumba Gold and ...ZZZZ (sleep better)

Trying something new is difficult. Why not check out a schedule, find programs that interest your mom and then hang out with her there for a couple of hours, twice? I'll bet she goes the third time without you.

44   Bit by painful bit, Alzheimer's stole from us

A thief came and stole from us. This is one thief that you can't arrest. His name is Alzheimer's.

It started about five years ago. At first, it was little things. Sometimes, Dad would be missing a piece of memory. "Alz" would take odds and ends. Just enough to start making us question if something was gone.

Was it just that the new car had such a fancy computer that you had to have a teenager around to run it, or was it something more? So we traded the car back in and bought an older model - one that had a key and had buttons on the dashboard, instead of a touch-screen. Some of Dad's confidence returned.

But not enough.

Dad knew that the thefts were taking place, but didn't let on. "Alz" snuck around with Dad everywhere Dad went; grabbing a memory out of life. What month is it? What is a fork for? It got progressively worse.

Mom took on the challenge to keep Dad as strong and complete as possible. She encouraged him to exercise both his brain and his body. He did. Eventually, Dad got tired.

One day last January, Dad received a small check in the mail, so naturally he wanted to deposit it. The problem was that it was five degrees below zero, and Dad forgot his coat. Having no car anymore, he decided to walk to the bank. He also forgot how to get there. Thank goodness that someone found him and brought him home.

That was that. Dad could no longer live safely at home.

Guilt. Placing someone in a secure community is hard; even when you know it is right. The heart says no. The mind tells you that there is only one real choice.

It was hard on Dad too, but he kept a brave face. Through his journey, he taught us kindness and compassion. His disease brought us closer together as a family.

At the end, "Alz" stole Dad's memory of how to breathe.

As the spirit left Dad, something new took its place. The worry wrinkles on his face fell away. Peace.

Now *we* get to forget. We forget the fear we saw when Dad knew what was happening but couldn't stop it. We forget the fear he had later when he didn't know what was happening.

Now we are free to remember what was. We get to remember all the good times. We laugh over stories of our exploits with Dad. Friends have shared their tales of how much fun they had with Dad. He was the guy everyone wanted to be with.

Memories - that is what Alzheimer's took from Dad.

Memories – that is what we have left to keep Dad warmly in our hearts. And we are full of that warmth.

Now it is January again. Is it only a year later?

Mom's favorite saying is "If you didn't laugh, you'd cry and laughing is just more fun." Over the past year, there have been many reasons to cry. Now, bit by bit, we've started to laugh again.

45   Give the gift of an old memory

Do you love Facebook more than you love Grandma?

No? Do your actions show it?

Amazingly, we spend more time posting life's moments to folks that we aren't related to than we do to those who gave us life.

Who are you friends with on FB? Some are people you hardly have any connection with anymore; people from high school who even live in other states; neighbors, "acquaintances".

We have this secret world that many of our grandmas don't see.

Maybe you are hooked on updates. Well, so is she!

This may be hard to believe, but there was life BFB (Before Facebook). Once upon a time, we would share memories by actually talking and reminiscing. We called Grandma every week to say "hi" and updated her on our life. We took pictures and then printed them off. We selected "duplicates" so we could give one to that special lady who loved to see them, and we kept one for ourselves.

Nowadays, we continue to take pictures. Lots of them. We may take 30 pictures of our wonderful experiences. We share them with anyone on FB who will look. Then we get lazy. We don't go any further. We don't print them off anymore. We don't even keep any of them for ourselves or our legacy.

You know how fun it is when FB shows you a memory, right? When they show you a picture from 6 or 8 years ago, you enjoy it all over again. True? They do that because they know it brings a real smile to you, and you even enjoy re-sharing it. It keeps you engaged with FB.

Do you know who is left out of your world? Grandma! She sits at home and doesn't see any of your cute pictures of the grandkids, nor your laughing comments about your dog, your trip nor even the updates about your cooking disasters. And you wonder why she is lonely.

There is joy in sharing memories.

Let's combine the old and the new. Here are some ways you can do it.

How many hours a week do you spend playing games on your cell phone or computer? 10? 20? Be honest.

Give the gift of an old memory: Skip a week of League of Legends or Solitaire. Instead, spend that time at Grandma's going through her scrapbooks together and reminiscing. You really do have time.

Don't live near her? Spend an hour on the phone sharing your week.

Give the gift of a newer memory: Actually print off those FB pictures once a month, buy some stamps and mail them to Grandma. Make it a habit. Wow! She would really start looking forward to the mail!

How about printing off one of those little Shutterfly or Walgreens books for her? What a treat. My daughter gave me one for my birthday. It is a keeper!

One more thing... You can also give the gift of making a new memory. When is the last time you did something memorable together? Do it now. Before there are no tomorrows.

46   Thirty minutes that changed a life forever

Lori Coonen from Living My Legacy shared this experience with me:

"My story begins with a death. And while that may not sound like the best of introductions to a tale of hope and promise, it is in fact the perfect bookend to a life-changing experience that was made possible for one family.

"During my 'Legacy Journaling' class at an assisted living facility, I offered to record for students who had difficulty typing. Sam took me up on the offer. Before Christmas, I sat with Sam for 30 minutes. In our brief time together, his focus was on sharing the details of his career path. I recorded our conversation and burned a CD so that Sam could share his stories with his family.

"In January, I received a call that my student, Sam, had died.

"I attended the visitation and after waiting in the long line, I was finally able to talk to Sam's widow, Joan, with her children standing next to her. She told me that in the final hours of Sam's life, the entire family was gathered around his bed as Sam lay there with his eyes closed – for several days he had been lying motionless. As they were gathered, she asked one of her sons if he could play the CD of Sam's conversation that we had recorded. Joan hadn't yet listened to it.

"Then a smile appeared on her face. Joan said Sam's whole family listened as the conversation played – Sam was sharing the highlights of his career path, the specific experiences and the lessons he learned. For 30 minutes Sam's wife and children sat beside him, holding his hands and listening to his stories. They were 30 perfect minutes.

"Joan and each of the children thanked Sam for the wonderful gift of the recording. Next, Joan told me, Sam's eyes opened, and he briefly gazed upon the faces of his family. It was as if he had struggled to hold onto his life just long enough to share this last gift, Joan said. And when the gift at last was delivered and he knew he sounded okay on the recording (she joked), he was ready to give up the fight.

"Each child thanked me for the opportunity that I had provided for their father to share his story – it meant the world to them.

"How many parents and grandparents are out there today, waiting and anxious to share their life experiences, lessons and values with their families? Would it be valuable to you to know the 'best' of that person has been preserved in such a way that it will lift up, educate, motivate and guide generations of the family to come?

"Give the gift of time to your father, mother, grandparent, or someone who inspires you. Offer to document their important stories and celebrate their Legacy. Be sure to take the next step and share them with the rest of the family."

You can read more of Lori Coonen's ideas at http://wwwLivingMyLegacyUSA.com/

Living My Legacy

PS. Note from a reader: "My only addition is to not wait too long. Sometimes old age/dementia steals some of the wonderful details/stories/memories. Do it soon.

47   Readers are invited to share ideas on loneliness (1 of 3)

The headline in the Post Crescent caught my eye: "Britain gets first-ever Minister for Loneliness".

My immediate thought was "Wow! How do we get one?"

This is not just a British problem. It sounds like something we could use help with, right here in Appleton - Fox Cities area. When I am out and about, it is achingly clear that many of our senior folks here are facing loneliness, too.

If we had our own Minister of Loneliness, what suggestions would we give them?

That story in the paper went on: *"Britain appointed its first-ever minister to combat loneliness, a problem the government says affects more than 9 million people in the country who always or often feel lonely.*

'For far too many, loneliness is a sad reality of modern life,' Prime Minister Theresa May said Wednesday in a statement. 'I

want us all to confront this and take action to address loneliness endured by the elderly, by caregivers, those who have lost loved ones — those with no one to talk to or share their thoughts and experiences with.'"

A Minister of Loneliness. Let's take a look at this.

We are not talking about being alone. Many people choose to be alone. That is not the same as being lonely.

We hear over and over from seniors that they want to stay in their house. Some are quite adamant about it. In the past several months, I have listened to discussions by several local organizations as they have asked how they can help make that happen; searching for ways they can enable seniors to stay in their house. Your community is looking for solutions for you.

I have to wonder if helping people stay in their house is a solution. What do you think?

It is time for you, our senior readers, to contribute to the next Transitions column.

Please give your input. Let's get a discussion going. Pick up a pen or log on to your computer. Write to me at: Transitions With Jean, 2301 W. Everett St., Appleton WI 54914 or e-mail: Jean@TransitionsWithJean.com

Here are some questions to share your views on:

- What are some obstacles that you face, that keep you from overcoming a lonely situation?
- What specific actions can we, in your community, do to help?
- If you are already doing things to combat loneliness, what are they? Please share your ideas with others.
- What suggestions would you have for a Minister of Loneliness?

In that article about Britain, their government said: *"about 200,000 seniors have not had a conversation with a friend or relative in more than a month, and up to 85% of disabled 18- to 34-year-olds feel lonely."*

Next time, we'll share some of your responses. We won't use your name. Let's get an exchange of ideas started. Perhaps in our small part of the world, we might come up with some answers on how to help each other out.

48   Readers seek ways to overcome loneliness (2 of 3)

Last time, I shared with you that Britain is creating a Minister of Loneliness and that my first thought was, "Wow! How do we get one?" So many people in our community are achingly lonely.

Readers were asked to share their ideas on overcoming loneliness. The responses were many; so many that this will be a two-part column. Here are some answers to two of my four questions:

1) What are some obstacles that you face, keeping you from overcoming a lonely situation?

- "I am a widow with a married daughter and no grandchildren. I had been doing OK with volunteering, but a year ago I had trouble walking and that has changed my life a lot. I would like to meet others who are in this situation. I don't know if we could meet at the senior center or not."

- One reader told me: "I am very happy in my house. They are going to have to drag me out of here feet first." Then, in the next breath, she said "I am so lonely."

- "Moving into an apartment isn't necessarily an answer. This society is so mixed up. It seems that people are wrapped up in their own lives and have no room for anyone else."

- "I am single. Some women are threatened by a single woman talking to their husbands. I'm not interested in them. I just want social interaction with people."

- "Many of my friends have stopped subscribing to newspapers; this is how I learn about social activities that are free or low-budget and age-related programs."

- "Larger gatherings like church pot-lucks are just too hard for me to feel comfortable with."

2) If you are already doing things to combat loneliness, what are they?

- "I hope to stay in my home as long as I physically can. I have a close-knit group of neighbors. We help each other. I also go to exercise class at the library – we talk and laugh during the class. I use the computers at the library on those days that I exercise there. It is very convenient to have access to the class, the computer, and the books, CD's, DVDs all in one place that is centrally located. Very thankful for that."

- "Church may be a good place to start – call to see if they could use help in some way."

- "Exercise - get outside and walk in good weather. I never exercised before but joined an exercise group. It turned out to be a physical and a social advantage for me."

- "Do one "fun" thing every day. Something you enjoy doing. Hobbies are a way to make new friends."

- "If you can get out of the house, volunteer. There are so many places that need help, and it is a great way to be social and/or feel needed."

- "If you cannot drive, call "Make a Ride Happen." They take people to various places, not just appointments."

- "Offer a helping hand to someone else."

- "If you can, live in senior housing where there are planned activities with like-aged folks."

- "Use the telephone. You may have to reach out and call others instead of waiting to be called. You need to reach out into the community. People do not come to you."

Next time: 1) What specific actions can we, in your community, do to help? 2) What suggestions would you have for a Minister of Loneliness?

49 Readers share ideas on overcoming loneliness (3 of 3)

The last few columns, we have been chatting about loneliness. Britain has assigned a Minister of Loneliness, so I asked how we might help our seniors who are becoming lonelier and more isolated. Last month, readers sent in suggestions of what they do to keep involved in the community. I posed two questions for this month.

What specific actions can we, in your community, do to help?

* One suggested: "Are there is any adopt-a-grandparent type of programs in the Valley? That would be such a neat way to connect people. Who wouldn't love to visit/play cards/chat/befriend an elderly person in need of a friend?

* There needs to be more senior-only apartments for people who aren't rich, but also aren't poor enough for the subsidized apartments. They should be secure, all-in-one buildings so you don't have to go outside in bad weather, with an activity room

so people can gather, close to a bus and grocery store – so we can eat healthy. A big plus would be if it were downtown where you can get out and walk to many things if you want to.

* One-on-one time. I don't like group activities, but if I could sit down with someone for an hour a week, just to chat, it would be something to look forward to.

* On a regular schedule, call someone who is living alone. If we all would do this, it would help. Many are sitting alone and are lonely.

What suggestions would you have for our own Minister of Loneliness?

* Perhaps they could be a clearing house for the area age-related programs available for group housing, ride assistance, NAMI, etc. The Minister of Loneliness contact information could be provided to healthcare facilities; to Human Resources when working with employees struggling with caring for their elderly loved ones; to houses of worship who attempt to maintain contact with homebound or those living in assisted-living sites.

*We could establish a free hotline for people to call when they are feeling lonely. This could be staffed with volunteers to talk about whatever the caller would like to talk about; i.e. weather, sports, family, cooking, whatever they feel like talking about. This would not only be therapeutic for both sides, but friendships could be made.

Folks, there are many things already going on to help. Your community cares. The key is that you have to reach out to them, and you have to be willing to accept help. You say you don't want help from a stranger? I promise you – they won't be a stranger for long. There are programs at churches, communities, meal-sites, senior centers, YMCA programs, Goodwill's Neighborhood Program, dial 211.

"The best way to not feel hopeless is to get up and do something. Don't wait for good things to happen to you. If you go out and make some good things happen, you will fill the world with hope, you will fill yourself with hope."

- Barack Obama

50   A clean attic is a gift for the whole family

May is attic month.

Years ago, you were running out of room in your house, so you boxed up stuff and put it in the attic. You figured you'd go through it later. Do you remember that chair from Aunt Dotty that you put up there in the 1980s? The seat needed recovering (still does). Then, there is the trunk. You can't remember where it is from, but someone in the family gave it to you so up into the attic it went.

Boxes, broken furniture, pictures, chairs, Christmas decorations, who knows what! You haven't been up there for years. Your kids keep telling you it needs to be cleared out.

We live in Wisconsin. No one wants to work up there in winter because it is freezing, literally. And summer? Are you kidding me? It is 120 degrees up there in July. It would be cruel to do it then.

Now is the time. Make a plan. Ask someone to bring down all (yes, all) of it and put it in the garage. Can the grandkids do it? Is there someone who you can hire to bring it all down? Maybe you know a starving student. Resolve that nothing will go back up there.

Then have the kids take whatever they want. Don't be surprised if they don't want any of those "treasures". The reason you stashed it up there in the first place was that you didn't have a use for it at the time.

If the mice have been feasting on it, out it goes.

Bat do-do? Get it gone. Don't give it to charity. Those hardworking volunteers don't need to be grossed out.

The broken chair; who are you saving it for? Out with it.

Do you have some items and you wonder if they are valuable? Look up "antique buyer" in your city. If their phone number has a different area code, skip them. Ask two antique buyers to come and look at your goodies and make an offer. Any reputable buyer should be willing to write down their offer and leave, giving you the opportunity to sleep on it. Don't decide while they are standing there.

What they don't offer on, and the kids didn't want, should go away. Relieve your children from the burden of doing this later. Do not make them go through all the work of bringing it down, and then ask them to put it back up there. That isn't fair.

The plan needs to have a start date and an end date. Don't let this drag on. 1) Bring it down. 2) Pitch out the nasties. 3) Kids take things. 4) Dealer makes offer. 5) Balance goes away.

Let's finish by the end of May. After all, we want to enjoy being outside in June, not mess around with dusty stuff that now is in the garage. Get it gone.

Mother's Day is this month. Ask the kids if they will give you this gift instead of flowers, do-dads and what-nots.

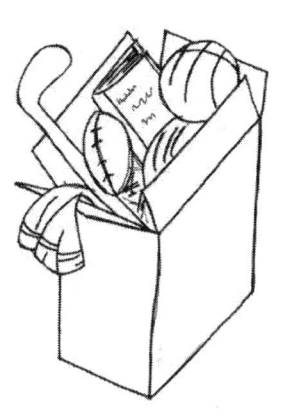

Note: If it isn't May when you read this, you can find a good day to get at it anyway!

51 Uncertainty of a new home can be daunting

Recently, there has been a flurry of news about refugees coming to our community. The Appleton-Fox Cities Kiwanis, a service club that I'm in, has been collecting furnishing to help the refugees set up their apartment.

Hearing about people who are forced to leave their homes and start a new life in a different place really pulls at my heart.

To some small extent, it reminds me of what some seniors go through.

Of course, the differences for refugees are dramatic; not understanding our language, looking different, horrific life experiences… and so on. But there are similarities.

Let me explain.   Maybe, together, we can understand both groups better.

The refugees grew up in a place that was home. They lived there all their lives. It was where their family was, and where they went to school. They knew their neighbors. Everything was familiar. They didn't want to leave.

Many seniors have lived in their family home for 40, 50 or 60 years. It is where they raised their family, knew all their neighbors, everything is familiar. They don't want to leave.

For the refugees, their world changed. Because of war, or an impossible situation, it isn't safe for them to live in their country anymore. They have to leave and start over in a new place. One that is unfamiliar, different.

For seniors, their world also may suddenly change. Their reason may be declining health, or death of their spouse. Their house may no longer be safe for them to live in anymore. They have to leave and go to a new place. One that also is unfamiliar, different.

Both groups are uncertain of their future. One would need the heart of lion not to be a little afraid.

They ask themselves what their new world will be like; wondering if they'll ever be happy again. They feel alone and unable to handle all that is coming at them.

This isn't people moving because they want to. Really, they have no choice.

When they get to their new home, they think they are alone. They feel lost.

In both cases, it is important to make their new apartment as home-like as possible. We want to surround them with items that take care of all their daily needs, but also items that define the word "home"; a place where they feel comfortable.

But more than the building they live in, we want to make the community that they move to a warm and inviting place to live.

How do we do that? Look them in the eye and say hello. Talk to them. Visit. Be friendly. Help overcome their fears of fitting in. Invite them to gatherings, or just coffee. Smile.

The good news is that often, after moving to a new place, folks say that they love it; everyone is so warm, and they feel such a part of their new home.

I guess they start to feel part of the community, rather than like a refugee.

Let's do all we can to say, "Welcome home."

52   Let's make a deal

This week, my friend shared something frustrating that had happened to her.

Dawn lives an hour away from her parents and can't get there as much as she would like, but she tries to talk to her folks often. Mom no longer drives and doesn't get out as much as she used to, so her conversations are basically about the neighbors and Mom's cat, Trixie.

Often, Dawn gets updates about the comings and goings across the street; stories about one neighbor who doesn't keep up his yard very well and needs to wash his windows. Mom also keeps her posted about another neighbor, Marie, including everything going on with Marie's health, Marie's kids, even how Marie's grandchildren are doing in school.

Dawn has listened to the status of Mom's tomatoes since they were seeds, as well as hearing about Trixie's latest exploits. She said Mom will talk ad nauseam about Trixie's stomach disorders, in detail. Gross.

Still, Dawn is an engaged listener because this is what is going on in her mom's life. She cares and wants to be there for her mom.

Yet, last week, a cousin called to ask Dawn why she hasn't been up to the hospital to see her Dad. What? She called Mom and was told, "I didn't want to bother you. Yes, Dad has been in the hospital for three days. He fell and had to go in an ambulance."

"Mom didn't want to bother me!" she told me, exasperated, "What is she thinking? I want to be bothered."

It ended up that Dad was dehydrated. Now he is back home and doing alright. Whew.

Can you imagine the stress that Dawn's mom was going through in those three days when they didn't know what the problem was? Not only that, but it must have been difficult for her to get to the hospital to see Dad and to have to face the worry all on her own.

My friend is not alone. I have heard many versions of this story from readers and friends alike. Their parents don't tell them important news because they don't want them to worry or because they don't want their child to take off work. "We don't want to be a burden."

Parents, we care about your everyday life and we also care about what is going on with your health. But one is a higher priority, and just in case you aren't sure, it isn't the cat's antics.

Let's make a deal. Bother us all you want, but can we agree that you will always bother us when it is a health or safety issue?

We want to be in the loop. We want to be your first call. We will be there for you. You aren't a bother. You are our parents.

Meanwhile, Dawn is back to the routine of chats with her mom and is happy to report that the tomatoes are ripening and will soon be ready for picking.

53 Game plan needed as kids divide up possessions

A few chapters ago a reader posed this dilemma:

Dear Jean: "Our parents have to move in the next few months.

How do we kids (six of us) unite and help them work through all the items they have acquired over their lifetime? Mom has put items on a table saying – take it, if you want it. We don't all live in the same city or state that she does. Some of us have an interest in the same items. Others have already asked and taken specific (special) items without the rest of us siblings knowing about it.

We have various personality types. Can you recommend guidelines (lottery system, putting names on items, having an in-family estate/auction…)? How do we deal with meddling in-laws or grandchildren's spouses stepping in?"

Answer: You said it yourself; the six kids need to unite.

It would be nice if this would happen by magic, but it won't. You have to work at it.

How many families have you seen torn apart by settling an estate? That is what this somewhat is, only better. Remember, you have the pleasure of doing it with your parents. You can share the memories and have a special time. Together.

Define what the real goals are here.

First, help Mom and Dad decide where they are going and get them there. All else should wait.

Second, your parents need the house cleared out. Instead of everyone pulling Mom in different directions, get your siblings to promise her that you will empty it, together. Pledge that after your folks are settled, you will all meet at the house for a weekend and get the job done.

Once you have made that commitment, ask Mom to stop giving items away.

The third goal is to keep family harmony. Everyone agree to stop taking things until you are all together. If someone suggests getting a dumpster, encourage them to be more sensitive to Mom and Dad's feelings.

From our readers:

Resoundingly, it was stated that only the six children and your parents should be at the house for the initial choices.

Get painters tape. Walk around the house together and mark a value on all items over $10. The group must agree on the amount. Often the items of the highest "value" have nothing to do with money.

Create a legacy list; family treasures that are special to Mom and Dad, that are to stay in the family and why. Can you find six?

Recommended ways of distributing included everything you mentioned. The means didn't seem as important as, in the end, feeling that it was fair. The hardest feelings arose when one person, no matter how well-meaning, decided for others about how this would be done. Define "fair" together.

Several recommended the workbook, "Who Gets Grandma's Yellow Pie Plate."

Be a leader. Before you start, do as one family did. Make a circle, hold hands and say, "Our love for each other is more important than stuff." Repeat as necessary.

54   A handy list for when a loved one passes away

The first time I lost a dear one, and had to handle all the paperwork, I didn't know where to begin.

Learning how to deal with the mountain of paperwork to officially complete a life is stressful and it comes at a time when you are already dealing with the emotions that come with losing someone.

Today's question: "Is there some kind of a checklist of things to do for a survivor? Things like dealing with the power company, bank accounts, Social Security, etc.?

The answer is provided by Attorney Kate Schilling, GWAAR Elder Law & Advocacy Center, Madison, WI. Shilling is happy to share her suggestions with us:

"When a spouse or loved one passes away, it can be a very difficult time for the family. Here is a non-exclusive list of actions that may help a family get started on finalizing the decedent's affairs:

- Look for a will in the person's home, a safe deposit box, or filed at the county Register in Probate office.

- Consult an attorney about the need for probate and payment of outstanding debts. A Transfer by Affidavit may be an option for estates of less than $50,000.

- Consult the preferred funeral home and find out if the person had advance burial planning in place.

- Notify the landlord in writing that the person has passed away. This limits the rental liability to two months of rent past the month of notification.

- Notify utility companies if cable or phone can be stopped.

- Notify Social Security Administration so that benefits are not overpaid, and so that dependent and widow's benefits can be properly paid out.

- Notify the life insurance company. Usually a death certificate is needed to pay out the beneficiary of record.

- Notify a POA agent or guardian that his/her authority has ended.

- Close out credit cards.

- If there is a surviving spouse and property is jointly titled, complete a HT-110 form to notify the county Register of Deeds office that one spouse has passed away. A death certificate must accompany this request.

- o Notify Medicaid Estate Recovery if the person received Medicaid benefits.

Note that many of these actions will require a person who has authority to act on behalf of the decedent, meaning the executor or personal representative of the estate. This is a very important role and GWAAR recommends that a personal representative consult with an elder law or probate attorney to ensure the estate is handled properly according to state statutes as paying creditors in the wrong order could cause personal liability on the part of the personal representative."

This from Jean: What a great list to cut out and save. Don't make your heirs play "hide and seek". With a little bit of planning, you can make this rough time easier for your family. By putting many of these items in one location and then sharing the location with your executor or personal representative, you will make their job so much easier. What a blessing.

55 Who are columns about? This time, it is Mom

Here is a little insight and then a message from my mom.

For nine years, I have been writing this Transitions column. My mom says people think it is specifically about us. My columns are not about Mom- they are about everybody; you, me, your parents, your kids, us. We are all sharing the experience of a life change, and we are all getting older.

Today, I actually am writing about my mom. Let me introduce you to Gladie Reimer Long. She grew up on Tayco Street in Menasha and moved to Appleton when she and Dad were married. She raised eight children on a tight budget.

Mom celebrates every day. If you meet her, she becomes your champion and wants the best for you. She has taught me to make the most of every situation.

Mom is a forward thinker. She and Dad started A-1 Moving & Storage in 1960. It was Dad's idea. Mom saw the possibilities, encouraged him to do it and together they took the leap. Mom was a full-time partner in the business.

Over the years, Mom has always been one step ahead of the game.

In later years, Mom and Dad built their dream home, ideal for hosting their many parties with family and friends. It was perfect for that time in their life.

Two years ago, Mom moved from the house into a retirement community. Dad had Alzheimer's and couldn't be independent anymore. He passed away just over a year ago.

That brings us to today. I interviewed Mom about the transitions she has made in the last couple of years.

Mom: "I know for sure that I wouldn't want to be anywhere else. I wouldn't want to be alone in a house by myself; I don't like that idea at all.

"Here, there is always something going on. All I do is step out my door and I have someone to talk to. Everyone is friendly. We talk and joke. I get into a good mood just by talking to them. When you come back (to the apartment), you're alone.

"I wasn't ready 4 years ago. I wasn't ready 3 years ago, but when the time came, it was the only choice. I had taken care of Dad as long as I could. I couldn't do it anymore.

"Everything fell in place. God was with me all the way.

"We moved here together, me here in this apartment and him just down the hall in memory care. It was perfect. I could see him whenever I wanted.

"Now I am here for when my situation changes. I might need assisted living or memory care, and I am here.

"Meanwhile, I've made lots of friends and we have a good time."

Jean: What I can tell you readers is that none of us children have to worry about Mom, she is more independent than the last few years in the house and she is livin'!

Again, you are right Mom. You made the right move.

As I said, Mom celebrates each day. For her birthday, she celebrates the whole month. So, if you see her any time in February, wish Mom a Happy Birthday!

56   Bloom where you're planted

Walking up to the front door, I couldn't help but notice that the house had seen better days. The shutters were weathered and in dire need of paint. The garden had random weeds overrunning the beautiful perennials.

In that moment, I could see back in time; a happy couple had lived there for many years. Can't you almost picture him puttering around the yard; fixing the trellis and painting the window boxes? For her. His bride of 50 or 60 years. Imagine her planting flowers and tending the garden, nurturing the new growth and fighting the weeds. This home was a team project.

Surely, they also annoyed each other from time to time, and they would bicker over simple things, maybe how to prune a lilac.

Don't we all?

Love grew there.

I also knew it wouldn't have looked so rough if they were both still there and in good health. Time marches on.

Then I gathered my thoughts and put on my smile. They called me because they needed help.

Reaching out to ring the doorbell, I noticed a little sign in the garden, just a cheery, plastic decoration with the simple phrase, "Bloom where you are planted". There was hope.

The daughter, Denise, answered the door with a quickness that told me she had been watching for me.

"Mom doesn't want to move," she whispered. "But we can't keep up anymore."

Apologetically, she overflowed with words, "We live 100 miles from here. We come every week, but I'm 64 and getting worn out. Mom never leaves the house and it isn't safe. We worry."

Meeting her mother, Marilyn, we chatted for a bit. She explained that she was moving to a senior community where Denise lives. She wasn't happy, but she was resigned.

"What is the hardest part about making the change?" I asked.

"It is so overwhelming," she answered, getting a bit choked up. "I don't know where to start." She added, "I won't know anyone there. All my memories are here. This is my home." Then, matter-of-factly, she said, "Change is hard."

Yes, change is hard.

Then I asked Marilyn, what is a plus for her moving? She ticked off the reasons: "It will be easier to keep house; my daughter won't worry, I'll have my meals every day." Then she got a twinkle in her eye as she happily finished with: "And I'll be near my grandchildren!"

Now we were getting to the heart of it. Folks are accepting of moving near their children, but those grandchildren – instant smiles!

Fast forward a month. Marilyn called yesterday. "You were right. I brought too much stuff!" she said laughing. We talked for a couple of minutes. I commiserated with her about how hard the transition was, and she finished it off with, "I'm happy here and I think it will be good."

I remembered that sign in Marilyn's garden: "Bloom where you are planted." And I smiled. Yes, I think she will be just fine.

57 Transitions trivia: Can you make the right call?

Dear Readers:

We have been sharing this *Transitions* column for many years. Have you been considering the ideas we've shared? Take this tongue-in-cheek test to see what you've learned.

1: The best way to help Mom clean out her house is: A) Inform her that you've ordered a dumpster, show up on Saturday and start pitching things out. B) Sneak into the house when she isn't home and throw things away. C) Make a plan together on how to clean it out. Be respectful of her feelings and memories. D) Ignore it. It's her problem.

2: Mom filled a box with special items of yours, such as your grade school report cards, your teddy bear, your old Mother's Day cards and the ceramic bowl you made in third grade. The best thing to do is: A) Walk over to her trash can and put it in. B) Take it home and then do whatever you want with it. C) Take the time to go through it with her. Enjoy it, share the memories and then take it home. The memories are more important than the stuff.

3: I've told my children that I've taken care of my funeral and gave them an envelope marked "My Final Wishes". When they ultimately open the envelope, they will find: A) I want red roses on the coffin. I would like my blue suit and here is a list of music I want played. B) I've made arrangements at XYZ funeral home. I want a traditional funeral with burial in our family plot. It is paid for. C) I didn't give them an envelope. The kids can do whatever they want. D) Why wait? Let's open the envelope now and discuss it together.

4: I've made it clear that I want to stay in my house. My children know that means: A) No matter what, they can make it happen because I gave them life. B) Let's try to make this work, but when it doesn't, I'll be open to conversations about what we can do to get me extra help so I can stay. C) Home is where the heart is. I can make my home anywhere that allows me to be safe and able to spend my time doing things I enjoy. D) They won't get me out of here without a fight.

5: Next Saturday is Dad's birthday. A great gift would be: A) Spending some dedicated time visiting (phone or in person). B) A fancy coffee maker. I think he drinks coffee. C) A new tie! D) A gift book of things I will do each month, such as January, change the furnace filter; February, do a puzzle together… Then do them.

6: Mother has offered to give you 100 bells from her 600-plus collection. A) Tell her you don't want her junk. B) Take them. C) Take them and ask for more. D) Together, agree that you will take away whatever she would like and that you can then keep, pass along or donate the items.

Certainly, there are no correct answers, but hopefully I got you thinking. Are there areas you might want to work on?

About the Author

Here is more information about me:

Business and Professional Experience
B.S., Business Admin., University of Wisconsin – Green Bay
President, A-1 Moving & Storage
Owner, Long's Senior Transitions
Columnist for Gannett, *Transitions*
Author, *"Transitions: Stories of how to help Mom & Dad with their stuff"*

Family
I am part of a large close-knit family. My husband has been my best friend for over forty years. We have two awesome children and four perfect grandchildren. We are also surrounded by brothers, sisters, parents, in-laws, aunts, uncles, and cousins galore. We are truly blessed.

Hobbies
Volunteering, volunteering, volunteering
Making a difference in someone's life brings joy. Put joy in your life by joining a club that is dedicated to service.

Speaker
Change can be overwhelming. I enjoy speaking to groups with my presentation entitled: *Making Choices for the Best Transition*. It is filled with ideas and inspiration about when and how to make a transition. Don't wait until you are overwhelmed. Reach me at Jean@TranstionsWithJean.com

Made in the USA
Monee, IL
04 September 2019